Carl Tighe has written two collections of short stories: *Pax: Variations* won him the *City Life* Writer of the Year 2000 Award, and *Rejoice!* which was nominated for the David Higham Prize and shortlisted for *The Irish Times* Fiction Award. His non fiction includes: *The Politics of Literature* and *Gdańsk,* which was nominated for the Silver PEN Award. He has had plays and stories broadcast on BBC Radio 4, BBC Radio Wales and Radio Telefis Eirin, and his stage play *A Whisper in the Wind* won the All London Drama Prize. *Burning Worm* is his first novel.

Praise for *Pax: Variations*

Designed to cause a real stir. Give the man a medal!
City Life

Dark and thoroughly thought provoking.
The Big Issue

A complex web of microscopic truths.
Home Cookin'

Praise for *Rejoice!*

A superb new writer... *Vogue*

Head and shoulders above the rest... shocking originality...
humour and horror within a tight and sparkling narrative.
20/20

Strong narrative cunning... admirable effects. It sticks in the
mind. *The Guardian*

A restless experimenter... elliptical stories, sharply observed
and efficiently told. *Publishers Weekly*

Most macabre. *The Observer*

Punkish. *Kirkus*

Vivid and disquieting. *Cahoots*

Imaginative and wonderfully written. *City Life*

Will make you quiver. *Quartos*

BURNING WORM

CARL TIGHE

 IMPress

Published by IMPress
26 Oak Road
Withington
Manchester
M20 3DA

ISBN 0-9538519-1-5

Printed and bound in Great Britain by
Rowland Digital, Bury St Edmunds, Suffolk.

Burning Worm

**memoirs, notes & diaries
of
Eugene Hinks**

**edited & introduced by
Prof Dr S.Mroz
Kraków Jagiellonian University**

contents

foreword

I was delighted to be asked to edit *Burning Worm*. I knew Eugene Hinks when, in those dark days long before the final collapse of communism, he worked in Poland as a teacher of English. As the fashion then was, he sported shoulder length hair, a drooping mustache - in winter a thick black beard - bell-bottom trousers, a blue/grey RAF greatcoat, and he was accompanied everywhere by an enormous old guitar on which he played complex, if rather obscure, American blues songs. I remember his contribution at parties with great affection. Some twenty years in advance of current western interest, he was keen to develop a taste for Bulgarian red wine.

In August 1980 Eugene Hinks, who by now must have spent several years teaching in Poland, accepted an offer to lecture in English at Kraków university. Although he did not know it, he did so just as the country launched itself into a major attempt at political and economic reform. But nobody really knew what the limits might be - democratic socialism, socialism with a human face or Stalinist totalitarianism with the teeth kicked out. Some said it was a *refolution* - peaceful revolution by creeping reform. Others claimed it was a cosmetic job, just another attempt to reform the un-reformable: fried snowballs. Either way, for over sixteen months the spectre of a Russian invasion and mass Polish resistance was a huge part of daily life. It haunted every moment, every waking thought and sleeping dream, every minute of every day. Only one thing was certain: as long as the power of the USSR was undimmed and Leonid Brezhnev remained in office as First Secretary, the limits of what could be achieved in Poland were very narrow.

Burning Worm

After the great shipyard strikes of August 1980 - the very moment Hinks accepted the offer to teach in Kraków - the Polish economy nose-dived: strike followed strike, right across the country, in giant factory and humble workshop, in farms, schools, universities and even in fire stations. The Party, unable to confront the union or its own reformists, incapable of accepting or initiating change, began to lose members and to disintegrate. Solidarność, reluctant to challenge the Party head-on, also began to lose control. Its membership was increasingly dissatisfied and restless. Various unpleasant strands of nationalist, anti-foreigner, anti-intellectual, anti-Semitic thought emerged - opinion not so very different from that of the Party.

A few days after starting work at Kraków university Hinks was quietly taken aside and asked to assist Solidarność. Specifically he was asked to listen to news broadcasts from the BBC World Service and to provide transcripts of any items relating to Poland. At the time Hinks thought it a very small request, but for the union it was absolutely vital to know what the rest of the world was thinking about it and to hear what western journalists had gleaned - our own press was still only just beginning to learn what investigative journalism meant. Hinks, without a moment's thought, agreed.

After this Solidarność, unwilling to draw the attention of the security services to him, left Hinks entirely alone. However, his relationship with the union, on his own admission, was uncomfortable to say the least. He was unfashionably critical of Lech Wałęsa on several occasions. The result was that his application for membership of the union was blocked by 'true Poles'. They said that although he was a worker he was not a

Polish worker. His application languished for months, went unanswered, was finally overtaken by the declaration of Martial Law, and now probably lies in some dusty military archive.

The Soviet failure to invade Poland was a sure sign of terminal decline. Already demoralised and in severe difficulties over Afghanistan, desperately trying to keep up with Reagan's Star Wars, the Soviet leadership knew they would suffer massively if they invaded Poland. Why should we knowingly walk into 35 million petrol bombs, was how one Soviet military official put it - unofficially of course. However, economic chaos, enormous queues, hunger marches in major cities, outbreaks of Hepatitis, Polio and TB all made it increasingly unlikely that the USSR would be willing to risk an invasion. But it all helped push the Polish military into imposing its own solution. The west, fixated on the possibility of Soviet intervention, did not notice for several months, the Polish military had gone calmly and quite openly about its preparations. On 13 December 1981 Poland, as Hinks put it so succinctly, invaded itself.

The declaration of Martial Law took the west - and most Poles, who had begun to believe union propaganda - completely by surprise. Inevitably Solidarność refused to accept the legality of Martial Law. There was in fact no provision for it in the Polish Constitution. And General Jaruzelski suspended not only the struggling and increasingly divided Solidarność, but also the corrupt and impotent Communist Party. Poland, after sixteen months of tension, crisis and near starvation, was too exhausted to offer much more than passive resistance to the military.

In some ways Hinks was very lucky. He had traveled much more freely than any foreign journalist. It was part of his job. He had contact with a wide range of Poles on a daily basis - contact not afforded foreign journalists. He could ask questions, pry, loiter, see things for himself. His are observations of 'the peaceful revolution' at street level: a narrative made up of recollections and stories about a society revealing itself to itself, turning itself inside out, recognising what it had become, seeing itself for the first time in over forty years. It is a portrait of a state and a state of mind. It is focused on the personal chaos and intense anguish of daily life, on the impact Solidarność had on lives, minds and ideas held for so long in stasis. This is not a story of politics, but it is a political story. The story is made up of the bits and pieces from which the apparently seamless fabric of history is written. Yet it is also, clearly, one of the many bits of history normally left out by professional historians.

In Poland we take *Burning Worm* to be an accurate personal account of the year 1980-81. Hinks was one of the very few 'outsiders' to witness these events close up: his knowledge of the Polish language and history, and his social contacts, made him an acute observer. But Polish culture can be remarkably inward looking. Naturally, few Poles would wish to identify wholly with Hinks's version or interpretation of events. Yet most agree: the simple fact that he is not a Pole, while it sometimes makes his opinions difficult for us to swallow, also makes his observation of us fascinating and, ultimately, more valuable.

Most of the people with whom Hinks worked in Poland have long since moved on. Some, sadly, are no longer with us. 'Maria', the woman in the book, survives. Of course it is not her real name. In 1980-81 'Maria' was a very junior lecturer in Kraków Polytechnic and I remembered seeing her with Hinks in Konwiwium, the university staff social club. Now she is a distinguished professor with several respected books to her name.

But what of Hinks? The answer is: nothing. Or rather, almost nothing. Nothing much for certain anyway. We are unsure of the date of his arrival in Poland - probably some time in 1973 or 1974. As far as I have been able to find out, Hinks had no family connection with Poland, so the fact that he could speak Polish is in itself something of a mystery, and his reasons for coming to Poland remain obscure. He always said he was Irish, but I do not remember him speaking with an Irish accent. One of my colleagues at the Jagiellonian University suggested he may have been of Jewish origin, but I think she remembers only his big black beard. Some said he was a spy. But for who, I wonder. And what would he spy on in a provincial classroom? My recollection is that Hinks had no interests beyond the normal ones of his generation: sex, music and booze. Of course, at the time none of us had any idea that he was writing - or what he was writing about. If anything this makes his achievement in *Burning Worm* even more remarkable.

But what is almost impossible to believe is that apart from the scattered fragments and stories that make up *Burning Worm*, Hinks appears to have written almost nothing else.

*

I have made extensive use of the work of Adam Żółty, Karol Kochanowski and Professor Harald Linge.[1]

---

[1] Adam Żółty, *Odnowa: a Hinks* [Kraków, 1992]; Karol Kochanowski, *Hinks - Pismy i Listy* [Warsaw, 1987];

Between them they have tracked down and pieced together all the material which appears here. As far as possible I have used the running order established in Linge's German edition. After a long battle with myself I decided to omit Hinks's account of his visit to West Berlin. While these scenes in Berlin are as vivid as anything Hinks wrote, and illustrate that he found life in the west as grindingly difficult and as stifling as life in Poland, they are, in the end German rather than Polish stories, and would sit rather uncomfortably here. Likewise I excluded his visit to Paris, his final encounter with the irritating, Marie-Therese, and the devastating outbreak of over-the-table fisticuffs that ensued when her family - a volatile mixture of French working class, Basque and Gypsy - met for Sunday dinner. This, too, I thought, only detracted from the main purpose of the Polish stories.

Prof Dr S.Mroz
Jagiellonian University
Kraków
Poland
3 May 1999

Professor Harald Linge *Hinks: Werke* [Stuttgart, 1997].

arrival

October 1980. Flying from London to Warsaw. Dark at three o clock in the afternoon. That was when we landed. Piles of frozen slush littered the runway. An indecent interval of face control, search and question, visa inspection. Released to search for my delayed flight south to Kraków.

An old Russian Ilyushin twin propeller. The engines were so loud it felt as if they were inside my head. Just before take off a metal panel on the underside of the engine slipped loose and swung by one rivet, exposing part of the engine. As the engines revved oil pumped out of a pipe. I called the steward and pointed to the problem. In a couple of minutes a workman with a ladder came along. He placed the ladder against the engine, climbed up, pushed the plate into place, gave it a couple of hefty whacks with a lump hammer and then went about his business.

Suspended above the muted glow of various Polish cities. It makes no difference where you fly in Poland, the flight always takes at least an hour. The hostess gave me a sugary wafer biscuit as if she were giving Communion to a diabetic. I slept. When I woke the No Smoking signs were on and the stewardess was checking seat belts. Out of the corner of my eye I noticed that the plate on the engine was dangling by the single rivet again and oil was spraying out behind us in a fine black mist. I quickly looked the other way.

We landed on the second bounce. Darkness. Slush. We could have been anywhere. The hostess announced our safe arrival in Gdańsk - a city at the very opposite end of the country from our intended destination. She did not bother to correct the mistake. It was only when we cleared the arrivals lounge that we knew for sure we were in Kraków after all. A man in a fur hat laughed and said to me:

- That's how it is in Poland. You never know where you are. Better get used to it.

- I know, I said. I've been here before.

But there are other things to get used to. There are the abiding smells of Poland. Cabbage, tea, shit, piss, tobacco, talc. These are the main ones. They hit you just inside the arrivals lounge and their familiarity is always a shock. They are the long lost smells of childhood. Later you catch the smell of boiled meat, herring, mustard and dill, fresh bread. On the streets the damp, sweet smell of brown coal in winter catches at the back of the throat, and there is the raw assault of two stroke petrol. And suddenly cutting across all this there is the sudden strong clear smell of violet scented talc. This too is Poland.

In the gloomy arrivals hall I buy a local newspaper. A tiny article, less than a column inch, tucked away in *Echo Krakowa* says that there are over 30 divisions of Soviet troops on maneuvers along the Ukrainian-Polish border. That is all. There is no explanation or comment. It is snowing. In the dark the stars gleam hard and cold The temperature is around minus 10 degrees.

Poland. Polska. The name derives from the word pole, meaning field. Polacy, Poles: field dwellers. The grey flatness of winter pins you, helpless. First and last the lack of feature, the long low almost unbroken horizon. Flat, flat, flat. Broken only by the occasional belt of woods and forests. Then the lack of colour. People reduced to dots in the distance, dark smudges against the sky. A landscape that forces you to your knees, clutch at the earth for fear you might fly off. The sky so huge, so grey, starts just above your head, almost at ceiling level. The stink of cabbage, piss and petrol clutches at your throat. At certain particular times of the year, you suddenly notice that day and night your soul is howling with boredom. You pray for something to happen to relieve the monotony. You pray to meet someone, anyone, on the road. The time between March and April is like that for me.

Where is it then, this place, this Poland? A General - one of Bismarck's, or was it one of Napoleon's? - said: Poland is not so much a place, it's more a state of mind. Out there somewhere. East. The East. East Bloc. The Badlands. Yet if you tilt Britain, or at least the map of Britain, on the pivot, the hinge, the axis of our world - London - then this exotic, remote place called Poland is suddenly no further than the Shetland Isles, only as far as Munich, Marseilles, Milan, Genoa, Bilbao, Turin. As near as Rome or Sardinia. Certainly nearer than the Falklands, nearer even than Gibraltar. And Poland has always regarded itself as the edge of civilisation, the eastern bastion of Europe, after which there was only.... the heathens, the barbarians, the vast emptiness of Russia. I have seen Poles returning from Russia fall to their knees and kiss the tarmac at Warsaw airport. Yet we know almost nothing about the place. It is a place we dare not go for fear of lurking monsters, yet it is our nearest neighbour, heir to all that this implies. But these things take some sorting out. So allow me my own good time. When was that, I wonder. My own good time. My own good time. And where? In memory? Perhaps. East or West, nowhere's best.

A two hour wait in the frozen grimy sludge for a taxi. Then a long weaving drive through the invisible countryside. At last the vague glow of Kraków. A warm flat. Anxious friends from previous visits. A revolution of sorts.

*

The first person I meet on my first day at work in Kraków is an old friend from a previous visit. Roman. As I entered the gloomy echoing main hall of Kolegium Nowum, he was standing in front of me. He was wearing his cap backwards. There was no mistaking his tall angular frame, his shaved head and deep set eyes - even his friends called him 'the skull'. Roman was walking backwards, as always, in some piece of street theatre of his own devising, holding in front of his face a cardboard box contraption with a toilet roll tube sticking out of the front.

- Roman, what are you doing?
- I'm making a film, what the fuck does it look like?
- Oh that's a camera…
- Of course it's a camera. So what are you doing here.… look into the lens please, this is an interview. Are we rolling? Yes we're rolling.
- I'm working.
- Things must be worse than I thought.
- What's the name of the film?
- 'Poland: The Last Days'.
- Gloomy.
- No, it's a comedy.
- Is it funny?
- A farce.
- Will anyone see it, apart from you?
- You think I have no film in my camera…?
- I think the film is in your head.

- Best place for it. The Russians would only burn it.

He put down his cardboard camera.

- What do you think, will they come?
- You never can tell with the Russians.
- If coming here is a really bad idea, then yes, they will come. But somebody in the Kremlin must have found a favourable aspect to the plan, which accounts for the delay.
- What about the Americans.
- They will shout a lot.
- Will they go nuclear?
- And kill the people they say they want to save for capitalism? Destroy their own markets? Very probably. They are as crazy as the Russians. But where would be the profit?

Roman handed me his camera. I raised it to my face and squinted, down the toilet role as if filming. Roman's skull, framed in the cardboard circle, gleamed in the dark. He smiled.

- Yup, the red light is on, we are rolling.... so let me see.... Yes, what will I do if it comes to a nuclear war? I will cover myself with a white sheet and walk very slowly towards the graveyard...
- The graveyard?
- To be tidy, you know. For those who come to clean up the mess afterwards.
- Why the white sheet, will it reflect radiation?
- Don't be a fool. Nothing can reflect radiation. It will be my funeral shroud. Every corpse must have one.
- So why walk slowly?
- Well, I wouldn't want to cause a panic.

Burning Worm

janusz

At a staff meeting, a character called Janusz turned to me and without introduction or preamble said:
- What the hell are you doing in Poland, man? You are not like the rest of us piss artists. You stick out like a sore thumb.

I assumed that this one of our teachers, someone who did not realise I was the new Assistant Director. I mumbled my excuses, smiled and moved away.

Slowly, over my first few weeks in the job, it emerged that there is a scandal in the department. A few weeks ago it seems Janusz took it upon himself to become Chairman of our Departmental Solidarność circle, and in this capacity drafted a new constitution, not only for the English language section, but for the whole of the modern languages department. At first nobody took much notice of this. But the new constitution, which appeared on the office notice board one morning, revised our relationship to the other departments, to the faculty and even the university and it not only removed the business of appointments from indirect Party control, it removed control of British Council appointments to a new committee.

While nobody ever said that the old constitution was perfect, and nobody wanted to have the Party approve appointments, the notion of changing our semi-independent status as a self-financing operation to make us part of the subsidised university structure, and put us under the control of people who were academics and knew nothing at all of the hurly-burly of the English Language teaching world was clearly a terrible mistake. What was worse, Janusz had no mandate from the membership to do this and undertook the drafting of the document without any consultation with the staff or heads of sections. What was even worse, upon closer investigation, no-one can actually recall how Janusz became Chairman of our Solidarność circle. Indeed, as he did not work in our department he should not have been a member of our circle. It seems he appointed himself. A full Solidarność meeting - only our second ever - is called.

The room is crowded and smoky. Janusz stands and opens the meeting by saying that as Chairman he is empowered to act as he sees fit, and if the membership don't like what he is doing they can remove him. Someone replies that as we had not elected him in the first place, getting rid of him would not be as simple as that. Another says Janusz obviously thinks he can behave just as he likes, but this is not the Party. This is democracy. He must be controlled. Someone else shouts out: Democracy is not about controlling others, it is about self-control. At the back of the room a voice says:

- I don't see the problem. If he wants to do it why not let him?

Someone asks who has seen the draft of the new constitution. It emerges that Janusz had sent copies of the document to just about everybody of any importance in the university. It is on Solidarność note paper. After a long silence, another speaker says that if the document is not withdrawn immediately he would resign from the union.

I ask to speak. I point out that Janusz, who was not elected to the post of Chairman, and who can thus only be considered an interim appointment, may well have overstepped the bounds of authority, by speaking for the department without permission and without consultation.

My boss stands up and says we should refer to Janusz in the minutes only as our interim Chairman, and that if he were to resign while we conducted democratic elections for the post of Chairman, it would certainly help us to repair some of the damage done by his premature circulation of something that could only ever have been a discussion paper.

Janusz jumps up shouting:

- Obstructionism! Technicalities! If you are making a proposal I insist you have a seconder. A vote! We must take a vote.

I reply that rather than force a vote it would be more gracious of he were to step down voluntarily. Somebody behind me shouts:

- Illegal is illegal. Janusz you are not our Chairman, you can insist on nothing!

Somebody else says we should hold an election now, this very minute, and that we should allow Janusz to stand against all comers. This is judged fair. There is general agreement. Ballot papers are improvised, tellers are nominated, three candidates volunteer to stand against Janusz. Then one of the teachers complains:

- How can we vote? We don't know if we are unanimously for or unanimously against any of them. Surely we have to decide that first...

Janusz hovers in the corner scowling and shuffling papers.

When the returns are counted, only four, out of nearly fifty people, vote against Janusz. Even his opponents voted for him. I feel very, very foolish. Janusz beams.

Next morning I arrive at work thinking the new statutes would be withdrawn for discussion by the whole circle. But when I arrive at the main bulletin board there is a crowd. The new constitution is nailed there like Luther's thesis. Janusz has not withdrawn the document, he has made it public. And there at the bottom it says that it is issued in our names. Next to it is a small notice saying that at the next meeting of the Solidarność circle the involvement of the British Council would be discussed and members would be asked to consider whether it was in the national interest to have such an important unit run and controlled by foreigners and foreign finance. And under that was a notice which said that in future Solidarność would review applications for membership by foreign nationals on an individual basis, and that until then all members holding foreign passports were to consider their membership suspended pending a full investigation.

I boil on up to my office. Nobody is bothered by these developments. There is an air of complacency. So he's done it. Yes. So what? That's what we elected him for isn't it? To get things done. Isn't that what we wanted, really?

Janusz wanders in, waving me aside says:

- It's only a draft. Only a draft.

The department secretary hands me a glass of tea, inspects her teeth for lipstick smudges in a compact mirror and tells me to calm down. Then she sets about repairing her beauty spot.

A few days later, pending a solution to this problem, someone wiser than me decided to recruit Janusz to the department on a temporary one-course-only basis, so that we could see him teaching and see how he fitted into our operation. That way, if we were called upon by the Studium management committee to make comment on the case it would be informed comment. I was against this, reasoning that it would give Janusz even further ammunition and would not mollify him but would lead him on in the belief that we were about to instate him as one of the directors. As luck would have it I pulled the short straw and Janusz was sent on my course. When we arrived at the school he immediately began hunting through the boxes of books. I asked him what he was looking for, thinking that such enthusiasm was unusual and that unpacking could wait until after what passed as dinner. Janusz replied that he was looking for the crate of vodka. He explained that it was widely known that we took a crate of vodka and a large box of foreign-made, available for dollars-only condoms on these courses. I laughed. He was puzzled to find nothing and assumed that I had these things hidden in my personal luggage. After this, as far as possible I avoided him for the whole ten days of the course.

Janusz knew I was avoiding him. And even though we didn't get on, one day he performed an act of kindness that thawed me a little. Janusz heard I wanted to shave off my beard. There is no icy wind, in fact the weather is fine, Spring is approaching, and the beard is hot. The beard can go. But I cannot find razor blades in the shops. Another shortage. Is that why so many Polish men have beards? One morning Janusz silently hands me a packet of razor blades. I shave. It is the first time I have seen my face in nearly ten years. What stranger stares at me in the mirror? Pale as parchment. I have the beginning of a double chin. Round my mouth are tight lines. It is a small mouth, with full lips, pursed and tense now like a little rosy beak. I only shave the once. Next day I say thank you and hand back to Janusz the blades and a packet of tea. The beard grows back within two weeks.

The course turned out to be a memorable one. On the second day we had to chain up the guard dog - a huge blond Labrador - because he had caught and eaten a chicken in the yard. Next day he broke the chain and ate another. On the third day he disappeared.

One night Janusz could stand prohibition no longer, and he drank a bottle of eau de cologne. I met him as he staggered along the corridor saying:

 - I had to do it you understand. I had to have a drink. I just had to.

Every time he opened his mouth a great wave of violet scent broke on the barrier of his teeth. We propped him in an armchair and advised him to sleep it off. He nodded his head and closed his eyes dutifully. We covered him with a blanket and crept off.

Apparently Janusz was woken a few minutes later by a student who had lost her room key. Janusz still in an alcoholic fog said he would sort everything out. The student thought he had a master key. But no. Janusz climbed up to the loft, out of the skylight down the steeply raked roof, and then down a drainpipe to a third floor ledge. Then he inched along the ledge until he found the window, kicked in the glass, opened the latch and slid into the room to open the door. His good deed accomplished he went to bed. In the morning he had a terrible hangover. He said even his shit stank of violets, but he had no memory at all of his climbing adventure.

The row about Janusz and Solidarność simmered for months, until the Director, Janusz and I were summoned to appear in front of one of the professors from the Management Committee to explain our positions. Janusz and I stood in the dirty crumbling corridor, stirring with our boots powdered concrete where floor tiles used to be, waiting for the professor to summon us.

- So what is Solidarność's next move? I ask.
- Now we are going to make Poland Polish, says Janusz. A home for real Poles, hell for Jews and communists.
- Do you think the Russians will come, I said.

Janusz turned to me, his eyes gleaming.

- Let the bastards come. We would love to fight them.

Overhead a military transport droned towards the airport. We both looked out of the window, into the night sky, and imagined. I said:

- Democracy moves slowly. I'm not sure you have time...

Janusz looked at me sideways and said, very quietly:

- You British will be the death of us with all your democratic shit. I am stockpiling petrol...
- I don't know how far you would get, the roads will be dangerous.
- I'm not going anywhere, you idiot. It's for making Molotov cocktails.

The professor running the committee was due to retire in a couple of months. While he looked like a typical old duffer with his carpet slippers poking out from under the desk and his hearing aid, he nevertheless had all his marbles and he listened patiently enough. Eventually he said:

- You know this whole question hinges, for this department, on whether Janusz *can* be Chairman of the Solidarność circle if he is not in fact a member of it. And that, of course, depends on whether you can legally allow someone who does not work in your department to belong to your circle.

Janusz said:

- I used to work for this department. A few years ago and I have maintained my connections and my interest in it. I was deprived of my post because the Party did not like me. They wanted to get their own agent in here. I was maneuvered out, sacked, unfairly dismissed for political reasons. Luckily I got a research post in Canada just after this, so I was able to apply for a temporary leave of absence. By rights, as a Polish citizen, and as the most highly qualified person in the department I should be Director. Instead we depend upon the grace and favour of the British Council and we have foreigners placed over us..... But now is the time to redress the grievance. I have repeatedly applied for work, to return to the job that is rightfully mine, but I have been blocked by the Party.

I thought: Aha, so now we have it.

The professor looked faintly surprised and said to Janusz:

- Are you seriously proposing that you, a person who does not even work in the Department should be appointed director?

- Yes, Professor. And I have here a letter from Solidarność supporting my claim.

Janusz reached into his pocket, took out a letter and placed it on the desk in front of the professor.

- These people are not even Poles. It is a disgrace that foreigners should be running key posts in the university. It demoralises us. It is a question of national prestige.

The professor knit his hands together in front of his face, drew a long breath and then said, very quietly:

- Dr Królik, you place me in a very difficult position. You see, for me this is not a question of national prestige. The British Council runs and funds this service unit. They appoint their own directors, they provide most of the books. We provide teaching space, teachers, a secretary and a phone. That is all. If we appoint you there will be no department. The British Council will not fund something they did not control. And if you think you would have access to hard currency by laying claim to this post you are mistaken. It is that simple.

The professor turned to the Director and said:

- Have you received any application for work from this man?

- No. Never.

He turned back to Janusz.

- And you say you were sacked by the Party.... ?

- Yes. I didn't want to leave, but they made it impossible for me to stay. So I applied for a temporary leave of absence, hoping that things would be better when I returned.

- You didn't resign?

- No. It was a temporary leave of absence. Forced on me for political reasons.

The professor reached into his briefcase and pulled out a document. He looked at it for a moment, sighed, then placed it on the desk in front of him.

- This affair begins to look like provocation. Either by the Party or by Solidarność. This is just the start. Let me put it this way, one of you is not doing Poland or the department any favours. If Dr Królik really is chairman of the Solidarność circle, and is empowered to act on the department's behalf, we will of course consider the new draft constitution. However, his status within the department is open to question. And it seems he has further ambitions. If this is an attempt to destabilise the work of the department then I have to say it has been quite successful, so far. But before it goes any further I have to give you all the chance to back-off. I suggest you leave things as they are for a while, get on with smaller tasks until we are calm enough to consider major changes.

There was a long silence. Nobody moved. The Professor tapped the document on the desk.

- Very well then. Dr Królik, if you are sure you wish to pursue this matter, we can resolve it here and now....

Janusz looked hesitant. He didn't know what the document was. Fear showed in his face.

- I have a grievance. We must eradicate the Party and foreign influence in our place of work.... I want my job back.... I have a duty.... a family... the national interest....

His voice tailed off. The professor slid the paper over the desk.

- Perhaps you recognise this, Dr Królik. It is a letter you wrote to the department. It says you are no longer able to work as a teacher of English because you have just won a scholarship to Canada and will be absent for at least three years - you were absent for four years, am I right? - and that as you have completed your doctorate in political science, upon your return you expect to find work in a political science department.... You praise the then Director, as I recall, a British Council appointment, saying how happy and pleasant your work in the department had been..... and you conclude by promising to send a postcard from Canada.....

Janusz's jaw sagged.

I never did get to the bottom of all this. Why had Janusz lied? He must have known that his letter of resignation would be on file, that his background would be checked, his file consulted. That is what bureaucracy is all about - communist or otherwise. Documents. Records.

I heard that about a year later, during Martial Law, Janusz was arrested wandering through a distant village singing anti-Russian songs. Drunk. Somebody heard him and phoned the military. Within minutes he was bundled into the back of an armoured car. He was hauled up before a military tribunal. They let him out on parole, but warned him that he now had a record.

janowice by night

It is very tense. The gossip is that meat and fat rations have been decided and will be introduced in January.[2] Each individual will be allowed 3 kilos of meat per month, including chicken, 3-10 kilos of fat per year depending on work classification. It has also been announced that Poland will save 10 million dollars by not importing the traditional Christmas carp. On the main town square in Kraków by dawn there were queues of 200-300 people waiting for cakes, sweets and chocolate, all of which will be rationed soon. One side street off the market square was blocked to traffic by no less than six intertwined queues. Everybody in a filthy temper, pushing, shoving, cheating, cursing, spitting.

Al Haig has again been on Radio Free Europe, Voice of America and the BBC World Service warning that Soviet maneuvers along the Ukrainian-Polish border were a cover up for the assembly of invasion forces. He estimated over 30 Soviet divisions had gathered on the eastern Polish border. Although Solidarność had won recognition for itself at the talks with the Party in the

---

[2] In fact food coupons were not introduced until April of the following year.

shipyards the previous August, when the union came to register its statutes in the courts, the courts had refused to register the union on the grounds that its constitution did not recognise the leading role of the Party. Solidarność appealed against the decision, and the debate dragged on.

Out in the countryside again. This time at the beautiful chateau in Janowice. This was to be one of our regular haunts, tucked away in the southern reaches of Poland. The village - just a weaving line of houses along the roadside - was set in the rolling valley bottom of the river Dunajec, surrounded by a low ring of hills and fields of cabbages and hay ricks. The river about three miles off was a distant ribbon of shiny gunmetal grey mud. The largest building was the chateau, the next largest was an auxiliary fire station. The smallest building was the local post office - a low, bright orange log cabin at the end of a muddy lane, where the kettle was always on the boil and where most of the villagers congregated for a chat and a glass of tea. The other shops in the village were a metal ware centre which was permanently shut, a grocery store where the assistants stood around with nothing to do because the shelves were empty, and a woolen goods shop which stocked only winter underwear and brightly coloured T-shirts. I bought two.

The chateau was a magnificent white building set in its own ornamental garden with a wide sweep of gravel approach, a triumphal double staircase at the front entrance, and a tower to one side. Rumour had it that there was a ghost in the tower. The building belonged to Kraków Polytechnic who used it as a study centre for students and academics. Before the war it had been owned by the Janowicki family and had been the centre of a modest estate the size of a small English county. The

Nazis had turned the dining hall into a stable, even though this meant they had to install special ramps to get their horses past the staircase. Such is the logic of racial superiority. Over the dining hall and the main staircase there hung huge chandeliers of Bohemian crystal.

After the evening meal of liver and potatoes - my first real food for several days - we canceled classes and assembled to watch the TV news. After a long speech the judge announced that the court of appeal had decided to register Solidarność after all. The room erupted in cheers, wild dancing and singing. Bottles of sulphurous apple wine were passed around, and slowly people began to filter away to discuss the news in small groups. Now, having gained recognition, people were worried this decision might prompt a Soviet invasion.

Things had just begun to quieten down when we realised that one of our number was asleep at the back of the room. It was the Professor of Aesthetics. With her Solidarność badge prominent on her cardigan she had snoozed through the whole drama. We jogged her elbow gently. She opened her eyes, rubbed her face and then staring hard at us said:

- Well, are those Solidarność sons of bitches arrested or what?

The lights went out. Once again we were in the grip of a power cut. They had become so frequent over the previous month that we had placed candles around the building at key spots rather than struggle to locate them anew each time. Within a minute or so, the candles were lit and regular evening classes were abandoned. We sat around for half an hour and slowly realised that the power was not going to resume for a while yet. Unbidden all but one of the precious candles were doused. Slowly everyone gathered around the single candle in the main hall.

Małgosia began to talk quietly to the woman sitting next to her. It was a conversation that had been pursued on and off for a couple of days, and for once - on the surface at least - it appeared that it was not about Solidarność, the leading role of the Party, the shortage of childrens' shoes or the economic crisis in general. Małgosia was a distinguished and well published anthropologist whose books had earned her a grudging respect from the academic community. She had just returned from a field trip to Afghanistan, was a skillful and fluent speaker in both English and Polish. Soon a circle had gathered about her. As usual there were no interruptions.

Małgosia had a husband. Their rows were public knowledge. Her husband enjoyed basking in the reflected glory of his wife's intelligence, but aided her efforts not a jot. It was a common setup. Like most Polish men he expected his wife to look after the home, do the cooking and cleaning, to stand in line for shopping, bring up their son, hold down a demanding university post and keep up a steady stream of bread and butter publications, while all he seemed to do was bring home a loaf of bread once in a while, read the newspapers and slide into the local bar for a vodka on his way home from work. Someone showed me a popular poem on this theme. There were several versions of the poem doing the rounds. I started a translation of two or three different versions, lost the original but carried on with the poem. I took a very free approach to the idea of rendering it in to English. But now I no longer know what came from the original version, and which bits were mine:

Burning Worm

At dawn I am the early bird
that wakes the family
I am the cave bear
chasing them out
to work and school
I am an elephant remembering
where and what to buy
I am a patient beast, a horse [or ass]
that waits seven hours in the queue
to get what? A lump of sugar
And then I am a camel laden
with parcels and packages
to keep my family together
at the school gate I am
a lioness fighting for her cubs
at dusk, a bower bird to keep
the home beautiful and clean
a squirrel hoarding and planning
for the future; and at night
my husband requires me a splay legged mare
snorting lust to his stallion will
My tigress lover, he says
but I must sleep, for tomorrow at dawn...

Małgosia was no different from most other Polish women
except perhaps in the degree of her personal achievements,
in the ferocity of her intelligence and resistance to the
position of women under Socialism. Małgosia spoke from
the circle of flickering candle light to an audience which,
apart from the reflected glint on a circle of Solidarność
lapel badges, remained unseen in the gloom.

 - Of course you can be sure that the Western press has
simplified the situation no end. There are photographers

everywhere, taking beautiful pictures of the noble *mujahedine* in their struggle against the awful Russian invaders. And the *mujahedine* are so photogenic in their long scarves and funny hats and beards. But the Russians.... well they are just peasants, lumpy, well-meaning perhaps, totally lacking in imagination, but not at all photogenic. And that's very important to the West, probably more important than any of the political issues. How do these people look? Of course it's all much more complex than that, and I can't say that our own press hasn't simplified things too. I have to put my professional concerns to one side for a moment here. I have to speak as a woman.... While the *mujahedine* demand our sympathy for their national struggle - and as Poles we know only too well what this means - at the same time we have to see very clearly what it is exactly they are struggling to restore and maintain. They want a Muslim society. Muslim. That means they are fighting to retain a social and religious system that is nothing more than a backward, reactionary, male dominated society, a straight-jacket for women. In most Muslim societies the place of women is in the back room, in the kitchen, with the children, behind a little black mask. They say that they are protecting women from the world and that they only behave according to Koranic Law, that they respect women, that they are obliged to respect women...

Her flow of memory and story were a delicate balancing act, made possible only by the flickering candle flame. Not forty miles away Russian tanks, probably manned by veterans of Afghanistan, were massing along the Polish borders. If there was one thing her Polish audience wished to hear it was that resistance to Communism was romantic, noble, inspired, popular with the West. If there was one thing they did not wish to hear about it was the failings of the anti-Russian forces. They did not want to know that, as if by default, the Russian invasion of Afghanistan possibly had some sort of double aspect. They wanted simple tales of right and wrong, tales of Russian defeat, of humiliating retreats, of arrogance and pride humbled by provincial mountain men.

The lights flickered and came back on. The audience, the intimacy of the dark now broken, blinked, stretched, yawned and slowly dispersed. Małgosia said:

- It must be strange for you, listening to Poles speak about Afghanistan.

- I'm getting quite an education this year, I said. One way or another.

Małgosia laughed.

- Yes. Poland is your Afghanistan... She pulled back the heavy curtain and searched the sky.

- No stars, she said. There is husbandry in heaven.

- Hamlet, I said, a little startled.

- Yes, a good old Polish play.

Małgosia pinched out the candle flame between her fingers and we watched the smoke coil toward the chandelier.

It was still too early to go to bed. I decided to go out for a walk. As I ambled along the village dogs began to howl ahead of me, and several drunks reeled across the road into the fields. The ban on alcohol meant that anybody who had a source was immediately noticeable in that year of prohibition. I turned off the road onto a lane, trying to work back along their route, to establish where they had come from.

I stalked cautiously through the mud. At the rear of the Church I saw a door standing open, and before the door a small orderly queue of farm workers. They stepped up in turn and handed over a fist of notes. The village priest as if conducting communion, was handing out bottles to his parishioners. Turning from the priest the farmers twisted the tops from the bottles and before they reached the muddy lane their Adam's Apples were bobbing noisily. Some squatted there in the lane and continued to drink, others after a slug to see that it was the real stuff, tucked their bottle into a pocket and went elsewhere.

One of the drinkers called me over and offered me a drink. A sudden shaft of yellow moonlight showed a long crust of dried blood down the side of his nose. I was close enough to smell that this was not vodka. This was *Bimber*. Moonshine. *Samogon*. Its own tail. Polish *poteen*. Lethal under any name. I declined the offer saying that unfortunately my health would not allow it. The farmer shrugged, assured me life was a bitch-mother and took a long slug.

The priest tidied up the pile of notes. He called out to ask if I wanted to buy. I said no, I was merely a tourist out for a walk. He closed the door plunging the drinking party abruptly into darkness. Someone raised a toast to Holy Mother Church and the blackness was filled with hoarse laughter and the steady glug-glug of serious drinking.

ela

We met in a crowded tearoom, not far from the town hall. She was introduced to me as Ela, and I was told that she was something to do with printing and publishing. Her escort ordered tea with strawberry jam in it, and our conversation lapsed until the order arrived. Ela explained that this was tea Russian style, and her long, deep crimson fingernails tapped on the side of the glass. She had elegant fingers and wore several rings that I suppose must have been real gold. Even though the tearoom was steamy she kept her huge white fur hat on. She wore a brown sweater, and jeans so tight they looked as if she had sprayed them on that morning. I don't think I met many Polish women so poised, so fresh, so confident and so delighted by the power of their sexuality. She fascinated me. Her make up was heavy, but perfectly applied. And I must have been staring because suddenly she looked at me with wide open brown eyes and flashed a magnificent smile. I flushed, mumbled and looked at the stained glasses set into the wall. We both knew that I was completely at her disposal. As the Poles say, under the slipper.[3] While her escort paid the bill she said to me:

- How old are you?
- Thirty. Why?
- I'm twenty seven,' she said, as if this was an answer.

Her escort returned and helped her into an expensive and almost floor-length fur coat. She shook me by the hand as if she was doing me a favour and then the pair of them left arm-in-arm. It was as if someone had turned out the lights.

A few days later I returned home to find a note pinned to my door.

- Would you like to see a banned play? Very secret. Ela.

There was no return address or phone number. I took a shower, ironed a shirt and waited. Only half the female population of Poland is called Ela, but I had no doubt who

---

[3] Slightly misused Polish idiom. 'Under the slipper' actually means 'hen pecked'.

it was. The only puzzle was how she had managed to get hold of my home address. Two hours later Ela arrived. She wore a different fur hat and a different fur coat, but her jeans were as ectodermic as before. Downstairs we climbed into her car - parked in a clearly marked no parking zone - and with a smile at a hovering milicja-man we zoomed off. Dodging trams, she explained that we were to see a preview of a production of a play called *Rzeżnia*.[4]

- Mrożek is one of our best playwrights and also a great cartoonist. We all love him dearly, even though he lives abroad. He is a great national hero, but rarely performed alas. A great pity.[5]

She sighed to emphasise the sadness and forced her way across and round a red traffic light.

- Were you ever a rally driver? I said, convinced her skills were extraordinary.

- No, but I had a boyfriend who was.

The performance was given in the basement of the Town Hall, and was for private and invited audience only. I noticed several of my students in the room and waved to them. They frowned though, and bit their lips before nodding in reply. Perhaps they thought my Polish was not up to this exercise, that the play would be too difficult for me. Perhaps they were just surprised to see me there. Ela said:

---

[4] *Rzeżnia* - slaughterhouse.

[5] Sławomir Mrożek [b.1930] began his career as a political cartoonist with the satirical magazine *Szpilki*. Joined the Party after Stalin's death and distinguished himself as a short story writer and dramatist. While he was abroad he protested at the Polish anti-Semitic campaign of 1968. He never returned to Poland, living in Paris, then Mexico.

- Tonight they will test out the play. They need to get the reaction of the censor before they go ahead with a proper production.

- But surely, I said, dredging up the few facts I had about the play. Surely the play has been performed before. I mean I've seen it in print. It's dramatic qualities must already be quite well known. Is this normal?

- Yes, you are right, but you see, the censor will be looking at the dramatic qualities in so much as they reflect and convey political realities and political qualities. Every production is different, so each must be judged on its own merits.

She opened her coat, fixed me with her huge brown eyes and leaned towards me. She spoke as if we were conspirators.

- You see it is a question of censorship. In this country everything must be passed by censor's office.

- Yes, I know that, but surely before too long Solidarność will start agitating to abolish, or at least reduce, the power of the censor...

She shrugged.

- Maybe. I don't know, but I don't think so. I know it is all a little crazy at the moment, but I think that when things calm down a little Solidarność will find the censor very useful. When Solidarność is a bit less.... youthful.... then I think they will see things differently. On mature reflection I suspect you will find that most Poles actually want to keep the censor...

I very nearly choked.

- What? But it's a pernicious system! Everybody admits it. And it's such a waste of money and energy and talent...

Ela smiled and leaned closer. Her mint-sweet breath tickled my nose.

- Sh!.... Yes of course it is. Of course. But you misunderstand the reality. You misunderstand the Poles I think. There is a difference between what they want and what they say they want. If you take away the censor you will make them all responsible for themselves. That is the last thing they want. That is the main problem with the Solidarność revolution. But of course they haven't realised it yet. Poles are worms. They don't want responsibility. History has proved this again and again. They need authority over them. The nation exists only in opposition to a threat: without that threat they all collapse. Also in a practical way, you can say that the censor keeps the milicja off the writers' backs.[6] They are never in trouble with the law simply because the censor makes sure they never say anything naughty. The censor is the writer's protector. You see if I'm not right. Solidarność

[6]Hinks uses the word *milicja*, rather than police. He is referring to the MO [Milicja Obywatelska, literally Civic Militia]. With the Army, Internal Security, Border Guards and Security Service, the MO was part of the apparatus of the State Committee of Security. It was not a bourgeois police force of professionals charged with maintaining democracy, law, order, protection of property and the apprehension of criminals. It was a centralised, armed, political police charged with maintaining the Party in power, monitoring dissidence and controlling the populace - if necessary by armed force. The MO fired on demonstrators several times, most notably in Gdynia and Gdańsk in 1970 [see pages 164-65]. However, during the Solidarność period it half-heartedly sought to distance itself from the provocative acts of the other security services and, as martial law approached, from the military. Immediately after the collapse of communism the MO transformed itself from a *milicja* into a *policja*.

will keep the censor as guarantor of its good intentions to the Soviet union...

At this point the lights went down and the play began. After about an hour I had to admit defeat and just let it wash over me. The language was much too difficult and allusive for me. I followed it in fragments, and yet one thing was clear: it was set in a slaughter house and the subject was meat. Given that meat had been at the centre of two abortive price hikes in the last ten years, both of which had led to serious disturbances and popular protest, the subject was potentially explosive. The actors, as far as I could tell, played down the political angle, but it was there for all to see. The performance itself was marred by a series of fluffs and dries and prompts, but the play proved to have a good start, a slow middle and an even slower end. By the time the lights came back up I was frankly bored. Ela too seemed disappointed.

- Very dull. Nothing special at all.

- What will the censor make of all this?

Ela waved a hand and laughed, then looking across the room she leaned in close and said:

- The censor will smile a lot, reassure everybody that it was a marvelous event, that it was very Polish in spirit and so on. Then the censor will wade into them, really take the thing apart, so that they all realise what a dangerous piece of work this is, and how if it was allowed on the stage at the present moment it could easily precipitate the Russian invasion. That every single line is absolutely dangerous. That's what to look for: lots of smiles and the flash of the stiletto.

- Oh...

- Don't be so unhappy. It's a game, that's all. The artists must all be made to feel important, dangerous. Their play will be cut to ribbons, and they'll appeal to higher authority, and the whole thing will drag on for months with discussions and alterations, and then finally they'll get their play without any serious cuts or changes. And they'll be happy. Far happier than if they had just been allowed to go ahead with it in the first place. They will feel that they've won a victory for Art, for Freedom, for Poland. You have to remember that if the play were passed uncut, without any problems, they would realise that what they have here is a harmless squib, rather than an atom bomb. It is the function of the censor to keep these people interested in squibs.

I was still digesting this argument when one of my students approached us, and thinking he wanted to speak to me I turned to greet him. But no, it was Ela he wanted to speak to. He gave a stiff formal bow and said:

- Madam Censor, we are ready for your comments now.

Ela whispered to me:

- My motto is smile a lot and cut like hell.

Then with a smile from ear to ear, still wearing her fur hat and coat she clicked her high heels across the wooden flooring towards the assembled cast. I heard her say:

- Ladies and Gentlemen, you should be proud of yourselves. You are a credit to the nation and to your profession. However...

I slipped out before she had finished.

christmas

At the corner they set up a huge canvas tank. They filled it with water and then stocked it with dozens of carp. This is the traditional Christmas meal in Poland. When you get to the front of the queue you point at the carp you want, they fish it out of the tank with a long handled net, wrap it in a piece of newspaper, drop the wet package into your bag and away you go. Carp can live for quite a while out of water. On the bus the woman next to me had a gasping carp in a string bag. It looked like it had asthma, like it was imploring me to tear it loose from the bag and throw it back in the river. Carp are bottom feeders; they dredge up all the muck. When you get them home they spend a week in the bath tub, swimming around without any food, just to clean out their system ready to be eaten. During this time nobody can take a bath.

I cannot face buying a carp and killing it. I wait, hoping something else I can eat will show up in the shops. It does not. I make a Christmas dinner of tinned peas and bread. I have been eating tinned peas and bread for over a week. I have noticed that with this diet I have begun to smell strange. I cannot quite place the smell: pear drops, nail varnish, fresh paint. My stomach growls. I fart a lot.

*

At the English Department Christmas Party, I was asked onto the dance floor by a tall, shapely first year called Anja. While I gave my impersonation of someone dancing she explained that although I did not teach any of the first year students, I was very popular with them. She said she had asked me to dance as a dare, though she also gave me to understand that it had been her choice to accept the dare. She glanced around the room. I caught her classmates grinning from the sidelines.

We danced for perhaps three records. Then during a slow smoochy number. She said:

- Is it true you are not married?
- Yes.
- It's not good to be alone. Why have you no wife?

I shrugged. This was not the time nor the place for intimate revelations.

- I don't know. Never found the right girl, perhaps.
- Or the right girl never found you. She laughed and pressed herself against me very carefully.

Later I bought her a coke.

- Are your friends watching? I said.
- Of course, she replied. And so are yours.

It was true, the head of the department, his deputy and two of their loyal assistants, one from the Literary Theory section the other from Linguistics, sat across the room staring. Anja said:

- You are not English…
- Irish.
- What is Ireland exactly?
- Very like Poland, really…. Catholic, potato diet, home distilled liquor, rebellious, partitioned, poor, rural…
- And you? Are you a wild poet, like I hear the Irish are?
- There's more than one kind of Irishman, just like there is more than one kind of Pole.
- You are wrong. There is only one kind of Pole. The boring kind.

She looked at the rows of teachers glaring and staring across the dance floor.

- I think we have just crushed a few toes, she said.

I had to agree. Within the rigidly proscribed student-teacher code she had made quite a stab at asserting her femininity, her personality, her rights and just about everything else that the traditionalists of the

English department found outside their control. She knew what she was doing.

Anja poured her incredibly sweet Polish coke and sat back, enjoying the upset.[7]

- In a few weeks I have my exams coming up. I would like to prepare for them. Would you help by giving me some conversation practice? I will pay you for your time.

When Anja arrived at my flat for her first lesson she was very late indeed and it was already dark. She was bundled up in a thick sheepskin coat and carried under her arm a large portfolio. She brought with her a great gasp of the sub-zero outside world. Her glasses steamed up. I made coffee. She wandered around my sitting room. She looked at the photographs on my wall, then switched on the lamp and swished the curtains shut. I gave her a mug of coffee. She cupped her hands and sniffed.

- I'm sorry I'm late, she said, unwinding her long scarf. But today I don't go to the university. I have no classes. That does not mean I have a free day. Quite the reverse. I must work. My mother and father think I have a job in a supermarket.

She unbuttoned her cardigan. She smelled of brown coal and lavender soap.

- So where do you work then?
- Not in a supermarket.
- That much I guessed.
- I work for a friend. An artist. He pays me by the hour. It's better money than in a shop.

---

[7] Both Pepsi-Cola and Coca-Cola were manufactured under licence in the People's Republic of Poland, though usually only one brand was available in most cities. It was said that the formula of both drinks had been adapted to Polish tastes.

She put down the coffee, laid her portfolio flat on the floor and untied the strings.

- Would you like to see some of his work?

- Of course. You don't think your artist friend would mind?

She laughed.

- I don't see why he should.

She opened the folio and took out a set of large black and white photographic prints. They were nude studies of Anja. They were not crude pictures. These had been done by a professional, someone who knew his job, who cared about precise effects. The lighting, the atmosphere, the skin tones, the grain of the print were all perfect.

- Of course I don't dare tell my parents what I am doing. They would never understand.

- I'm sure.

- I have taken you into my confidence now. You won't tell them will you?

- Of course not. I doubt that I shall ever meet them.

- Well, said Anja smiling. You never know.

I went through the pictures one by one. Anja, knelt beside me. I could feel her right breast pressing into the small of my back. I began to blush. I turned to speak, she moved to sit in front of me, her legs splayed. She took off her glasses. I noticed for the first time that her front teeth were crooked.

- You don't think that my breasts are too large do you? I hear that Englishmen like large breasts, but I don't like to think that I am out of proportion.

She took my willing hand under her cardigan. Through the cotton of her blouse I could feel warm flesh. She wore no bra.

- No. Not too big at all. It fits your hand perfectly.

I could not help it. I kissed her, tasting coffee on her tongue. She leaned back.

- My legs are very long. She raised her leg high in the air, over my head, her skirt slipped up to reveal that apart from woolen stockings and a garter belt she wore nothing underneath.

- And very slender too, don't you agree?

I muttered agreement.

She unbuttoned her blouse.

- You would like to compare the photographs with the real thing.

It was not a question.

I could feel myself slipping. In a moment I would be incapable of any sensible thought. I said:

- This is not another part of your dare is it?

- Of course not. Come to me. Come.

She pulled me towards her. Her knees held me. Summoning up my last reserves of reserve I said:

- Anja. A moment. If you want to make love, we will do it. Right now. This minute. But I have to tell you - I will not be marking any of the First Year English Exam papers.

Anja sat up abruptly.

- What?

- I will not be marking your paper...

There was a moment of silence.

- Anja, let's make love. We can discuss this later...

- Well just who is going to mark the exam then?

She was already gathering the photographs, buttoning her blouse.

- Mrs Kurpinska....

- That old cow! Shit...

- You could still come for conversation lessons. We could see each other…

Her scarf hung in the air for a moment and then she was gone, leaving only a faint scent of lavender.

*

I spend Christmas day staring at the wall in my sitting room. I have decided to build a house in my imagination. It is a special plan, with everything I could ever want. Not luxurious or flash, but very comfortable. I imagine that the wall is a screen and I move walls and beams, and sliding windows and staircases back and forth to get the best arrangement. I look up. It is dark outside. Snowing again. I am exhausted from all the mental exercise. I wrap myself in the duvet, sniffing my strange, high, body odour. I think of fried eggs and sausage. I start a conversation with one of the builders of my dream home. We discuss a cross beam. I stop myself. I am arguing with someone who does not exist. This will never do.

on sundays

Sunday in Kraków. It is snowing again. The temperature is around minus 10 degrees by day. My bathroom window was broken by the wind several nights ago; the janitor is very slow in repairing it; now I sit on the chilly seat with snowflakes falling on my head and shoulders. A snowdrift in my bathroom around my feet. Snow. Outside my window is a black tree. Stark and leafless against the snow. Crows perch noisily on the branches. I cut some cardboard to size and pin it over the broken window.

I woke this morning dreaming of egg and chips and tea with milk. Yesterday I found a tin of mixed vegetables in the cupboard, left by the previous occupant. Today though there is nothing in the house to eat. I manage to get out to the shops in spite of the snow and biting wind, but it is Sunday. Everything is shut. The streets are deserted. However, the little kiosk at the corner of my street is open. No bread, but I find eggs and - wonder of wonders - tomatoes.

At ten-o-clock there is a sudden booming, roaring noise from all over the estate. I go onto the balcony to find that everyone else is on their balcony too, whole families, dressed in their finest, clutching radios with the sound turned up full blast.[8] They are listening to the broadcast of a sung Catholic mass. This must be happening all over Poland: Catholic mass blasting from every warbling, crackling receiver, from thousands of grey Stalinist facades. And when that is over these families all troop off to the local church for a mass of their own. I wonder, if this place were not so Catholic, would it be so communist? And then I wonder the opposite: if this place were not so communist, could it be so Catholic?

The communal central heating system is not functioning. There is no water until four in the afternoon. Nobody can flush their toilet, and the toilets are those continental ones with the little stage where the shit just sits and stinks. I have the opportunity to inspect my excrement at leisure. It smells Polish now. The whole apartment block stinks by mid morning.

I spend the day writing letters, trying to watch TV. The TV set flickers constantly as the current is low, and no

---

[8] Catholic mass was broadcast on Polish radio up to January 1950. Broadcast was resumed on 21 September 1980.

amount of adjustment to the vertical or horizontal hold makes any difference. *The Muppet Show* on TV in Polish flickers past. Then a programme called 'How to Sell Meat'. The picture flips so badly I can't watch, only listen. Why is this programme being shown? Is it a provocation? There is no meat in the shops to buy. Is this one of the new found freedoms? I have to sit cold in my own home, with the stink of shit in my nostrils, my stomach flapping against my backbone, and listen to this nonsense!

Finally there is a power cut - the third this week. Without warning the lights go out. No heat, no light. No more reading. I move to the kitchen and sit with the oven door of my gas cooker open. This is my only source of heat. The cooker has the unlovely manufacturer's name of WROMET. I check the taps. The water is back on, and we still have gas. I decide to have a bath. There is nothing, absolutely nothing else for me to do. I would like to read but it is too dark. I light a candle and set it on the bathroom shelf. The tiny flame is thrown and magnified by the shaving mirror. Luckily my water heater is gas operated. I slide into the soapy water humming to myself: 'There's nobody here but us chickens'.

*

My flat is on the Azory estate, located to the north west of the city centre, just over the main Warsaw-Kraków railway line, next to paratrooper barracks. The estate sits on the main road to the airport. The estate is one of the largest housing developments in Kraków. It was built in the 1930s and symbolically named 'Azores' as a gesture of faith in the emergence of a New World. On my first day

I had walked around the district, studying my map. I'm no general, but clearly this is a strategic location. If I were the Soviet military planner what would I do? How would I set about seizing Kraków - a major industrial site, a communications centre, a main rail junction, an airbase and a military centre?

The city is HQ for the Airborne Division. In a ground defence role, the task of the airborne troops would be either to seal off the Carpathian pass from Czechoslovakia or support troops facing the Ukraine. Fifth column activities would certainly ease capture of the city, but if the Soviets wished to avoid protracted struggle they would have to seize the city quickly. That means knocking out the main barracks, taking the airport, straddling the road and rail links to Warsaw. Not far from my portent block there is a huge wasteland that serves as a local market. And at the back of the block there is a wide open space of heath and allotments. Both places are perfect for a paratrooper and glider assault. Night after night I lie in bed - listening to warnings of Russian troop movements on the radio - listening to the planes flying overhead, wondering if the rustling of wind on the bare trees is really the sound of the wind in silk. All I can think is: Shit, I'm right in the middle of a strategic position. So what do I do? I read.

*

I reread smuggled copies of George Orwell's *Homage to Catalonia* and John Reed's *Ten Days that Shook the World*. I did not trust Reed's book. He knew too much about what was going on around him. He understood everything the moment it happened. And somehow he always seemed to be in the right place at the right time. Perhaps he was in the right place every time and maybe that's what makes him so special. And maybe he was right about everything too. But the feeling of the thing was wrong. I could not put my finger on it, but it just felt wrong.

Orwell seemed nearer the truth. The opening sequence foreshadows everything that follows. His wound comes out of the blue and it is altogether inglorious. If Reed had been injured it would have been a flesh wound to his upper left arm - he would still be able to speak and write and the bandage would have looked good. Orwell's comprehension is limited to what he can see around him. Anything outside his immediate environment is shaky. The sense he makes of things comes afterwards, upon reflection. It is a sense he makes for himself and for the interested and equally puzzled reader. It doesn't feel like a fabrication: the confusion is too powerful. The scenes where Orwell looks down from the Barcelona rooftops into the streets strikes me as particularly accurate. He admits that even though he can see what is going on he has no idea what it means. That is real. That is enormously personal. There's no faking that. Here snap decisions are likely to be disastrous, and Orwell lets us feel that.

What is it I am trying to capture here? What I experienced was not nearly as dramatic as the events that Orwell and Reed capture, but somehow.... And if I could say it succinctly, I would not have to do it through these stories, by this rambling and indirect route. I remember Yeats's 'Meditations in Time of Civil War':

Burning Worm

We are closed in, and the key is turned
On our uncertainty; somewhere
A man is killed, or a house burned,
Yet no clear fact to be discerned.

That is it and yet, not it. It goes deeper even than that uncertainty. The confusion mounts, it is elevated almost to a principle of existence. There is no value in repetition, yet there is value only in repetition, in detail. There is a passage in Paolo Spriano's *The Occupation of the Factories* which seems relevant. He wrote:

> To restore the problem to its real dimension and to subject it to minute examination is not to rob the movement of any of its grandeur and originality, or to stifle in us all sense of the great fear of the bourgeoisie or the courage of the worker occupiers. On the contrary, it restores to them those multiple, complex features and that sense of anguished crisis which were properly theirs.

I can recognise my struggle in this. But how can I do the things Spriano speaks of when I know so little and I don't trust the little I know?

*

Once, on a Sunday, by some magnificent fluke, things went magnificently right: the drizzle lifted, the wind dropped, and I had bought several P.G. Wodehouse novels in English from the Sunday book market. I put them in my string bag and scuttled home. I was secure. Secure with a

54

good read. Secure in that whatever I read now I would be able to swap later. And there I was sitting on my balcony, my coat pulled up about my ears, the damp steaming away all around me as the weak sun rose towards midday. In my mind's eye I have Jeeves shimmering in with a cup of the old life giving amber nectar and a spot of E and B.[9] I'm surrounded by the whole tribe of duffers and drones - Gussie Fink-Nottle, Madeleine Bassett, Bertie himself. I laugh out loud. I laugh until the tears run down my face and my shirt front is wet. The kids in the playground below, splashing in the puddles, look up to my balcony and wonder if they should tell their parents about the strange man laughing. I feel sick, I have laughed so much.

*

But the invasion seems to be imminent. It always seems to be just about the happen. I decide to keep a bag packed with clean clothes, a bar of chocolate, a box of matches, a tin opener and a torch. I keep the bag, ready on a chair in the hallway. If trouble begins I can be out of the house in a moment or two. The bag stands in the hall. Every so often I take the clothes out to air them.

*

The lights come back on, very dim, at much reduced current. It is just about possible to read. Tadek has given me the typescript of a novel. He said it was a legal copy of a book which the author had been allowed to circulate for comment. It is Konwicki's novel, *Mała Apokalypsa*. Tadek said it was highly unlikely the censor would pass

---

[9] Eggs and bacon.

the book for publication, and it was likely it would eventually be published by Polish émigrés in Paris.

- You will enjoy it I'm sure. This writer is a very good observer.

With my dictionary I start to read. The opening paragraph is startling:

> Here comes the end of the world. Here it comes. It approaches you, or creeps up on you, your own end of the world. The end of your personal world. But before your world explodes into pieces, scatters into atoms, blows into vacuum, the last lap of your marathon is waiting, the last kilometer to your Golgotha. [10]

It feels a little too close to home just at this moment. He could have written this at any time in the ten years, even before Solidarność, and it would have been seen as a kind of desperate fiction. But now, after the birth of Solidarność, the unreality of Polish life feels so real, so normal. The sense that something which had died but had

---

[10]Tadeusz Konwicki [b.1926]. Fought in the resistance around Wilno, escaped arrest by the Soviets, studied architecture in Kraków, but never graduated. He joined the Party in 1946 but became increasingly disillusioned; awarded several state literature prizes, but abandoned socialist realism and then left the Party in 1966. Even the underground press felt *Mała Apokalypsa* [A Minor Apocalypse] should not be published in Poland: it was just too demoralising. By the time Hinks read the manuscript it had already been published in Paris, but neither he nor Tadek seem to realise this. In its mood and sense of the craziness of Polish daily life the book prefigured Solidarność and the events of 1980-81. It appeared in English in 1983.

not yet ended is all around us. Something died, but not quite. Something was born, but not quite. That is the feeling on the streets and in the shops and classrooms and corridors, on the buses and trams. The feeling is that something has already happened, but you just can't see it.

After reading I feel very lonely. If I had been able to find a job at home I would not be here. But I am here. Nothing warps like loneliness: loneliness warps utterly. I am so lonely I could cry, but the tears don't come. Just long sighs.

I switch on the radio. BBC World Service reports that the Soviet new agency TASS is claiming there were riots in the Polish town of Kielce. If there were then the Polish media failed to report them. Did the Soviets invent riots in order to get the ball rolling for the invasion? A few days ago I phoned the British Council in Warsaw to see what we should do in the event of hostilities. All they could say was 'We think you should be OK'. Tension is so high. They don't seem to be aware of it though. Typical diplomatic service types: they shuttle between the British Embassy and the British Council offices, their own little enclave. They do no more than breathe the Polish air. Beyond this they have no contact with the place, and certainly not with life on the streets. Standing in a queue would do them the world of good, I have no doubt. After this, I think a Russian invasion might actually be a relief.

a state of mind

On my way home I saw two militia-men approach a figure draped across the front of a tram stand. They were reluctant to arrest drunks because the treatment they received in the local drying-out tank was so harsh. I knew they would try to rouse him and send him on his way.

As I drew nearer I could see the man was stretched full length, face down on the concrete and that he was totally oblivious to us. The temperature must have been several - perhaps as much as ten - degrees below zero. There was a freezing fog. One of the militiamen called out to me as I passed by. Did I live locally, did I know the man, could I escort him home? I bent over to see if I recognised him.

- Hey! Wake up,' said one of the militiamen, digging the drunk in the ribs with his toe. The drunk did not stir.

I didn't recognise him from his crumpled profile. One of the militiamen said:

- I wonder where he got the booze.

The other said:

- With all that vodka inside him he could get frost-bite without even noticing it; he might freeze to death if we leave him.

They debated for a moment and decided to search for his papers. If possible - if he lived within their patrol area - they would see him home. But if he lived a way off then they would have to take him in.

The bulkier of the two policemen set his feet, gripped the drunk firmly round the waist, gave a grunt and heaved. As the body turned we realised that the man's face had frozen to the concrete slab. We shouted a warning, but the militiaman was quick and strong and we were too late. There was a pulpy, sucking sound and then the drunk lay back against the shelter, unconscious and mercifully oblivious to his injury. The burly militiaman cursed that he had blood on his sleeves, and then knelt in front of the drunk to assess the damage. He invoked Christ under his breath. His partner said they had better call an ambulance quick. The bulky one replied there was no hurry, in this cold the bleeding would stop in a moment. Looking closer he said:

- He's lucky he didn't lose an eye along with everything else.

I stepped away from the bloody mess on the pavement as quickly as possible. I could only manage half a dozen steps before my stomach protested. I clung to a lamp post, and threw up my meagre supper across the roadway. I heard the sweat freeze on my forehead. Unable to move, I waited. I noticed the second militiaman. A few feet from me, he too was bent over the gutter, trying not to splash his boots. He shook his head, mopped his brow and straightened slowly to look at me. His voice still thick with vomit, he said slowly:

- So…. you eat in the milicja canteen too…

*

The tram stood at the lights, waiting for green. The only sounds, the creaking of leather straps and breath freezing on the windows.

*

Driving back from the countryside in the bus. A difficult winding road. A thick carpet of mucky snow and ice on the road, a low drifting mist and then a sudden, hard blinding buffet of fresh snow. We edge over the narrow wooden bridge, the driver cursing that he cannot see more than a few feet ahead, cannot even see the rear of the bus in his mirror. The suddenly the driver hits the brake and we are all flung forward. The driver stands up in his seat, peers out, and then points to a spot just in front of us. A body is stretched out across the crown of the road. Two of our party, Marek and Wacek, are doctors. They leap off the bus and stagger against the wind to inspect what we are sure must be a gruesome corpse from some awful road accident.

They lean over the body and suddenly both recoil. Wacek turns to the bus and then mimes a man drinking. The man is not dead. He's drunk. Stinking drunk in fact. Unconscious. Looking round we notice that the corpse has collapsed only a few feet from the front door of the village bar. He is almost certainly the victim of an illegal homemade vodka bash. Between them, holding their breath, Marek and Wacek haul the body from the road and prop it in a doorway. Marek picks up a fur hat and slaps it on the drunk's head. They both look as if a sewer burst under their nose. Through the whizzing blur of snow we can now make out other scattered unconscious forms under a fine blanket of white.

Marx talks of the idiocy of rural life, but I wish I had their talent for finding booze. It's five months since I last had a drink. There is clearly no substitute for local knowledge, but I doubt that I am desperate enough to drink whatever it was they had found. Marek and Wacek return to the bus dusting snow from their shoulders. They shout in unison:

- He was completely drunk!

You can tell they are old friends. The bus groans ambiguously. Is that all. What an idiot. We knew it all along. Worry for nothing. We wish we could be so oblivious.

Burning Worm

*

I took a taxi home. Only after we had started moving did I realise that there was no meter, that the driver had no ID on display. In the dark I had mistaken this family Fiat, a private car moonlighting, for an officially registered taxi. I had always made a point of shunning these entrepreneurs in the past as their trade was illegal. At the very moment I realised my mistake a milicja-man stepped out of the shadows and waved us to a halt with his flashlight. The driver wound down the window and meekly handed over his licence. I had the impression that this was not the first time these two had met. The milicja-man opened the licence and there was a folded 100 złoty note. He took the note, put it in his pocket and handed back the licence.

- Well, said the driver.
- Well, said the milicja-man.
- Well, said the driver.

   The milicja-man shone his torch at me.

- And how does sir like our Poland?
- Very pretty, but very sad.
- True, said the milicja-man. Pretty and sad.

   We drove on. When we reached my apartment block I asked the driver how much I owed. He said:

- This is free enterprise. Capitalism. What do you think it was worth.
- Normally that journey is thirty złoties.

   He shrugged. I gave him thirty złoties. He looked at the money and said:

- But I had to pay the milicja. This is not good business.
- This is capitalism, my friend, I said. And you are welcome to it.

*

Jolanta told me my dentist was dead. We walked through the city gardens watching the pigeons, up to their ankles in sludge, fight their battle with the world.

- She was eighty-five, said Jolanta.

I remembered a series of visits I made to her in Gdańsk in 1976. On each occasion she apologised for having no anaesthetic. On the last visit she had only a little amalgam and filled my tooth with cotton wool. Her drill was an antiquated foot-pedal job, left behind by the Germans at the end of the war. Although I feared the worst, she never hurt me. Jolanta said:

- You know they gave her a high-speed electric drill at the clinic? Imported from Sweden. She refused to retire until it was installed and working. She just hung on and hung on. Sheer willpower. She wanted to be the first to use it. That's how she died. Faulty installation. An electric shock brought on a heart attack. She made a terrible mess of the man's mouth...

- You mean she was.... ?

- Oh yes. Right up to the end. She was drilling a tooth...

films

Just after Christmas I went with Maria to see Andrzej Wajda's film *Workers '80*, his newsreel record of the August 1980 negotiations at the shipyards. Wajda had not made the newsreel himself, but he had supervised, directed and edited the material. In effect he was the producer.

There came a point in the film when Deputy Premier Jagielski, who was negotiating across the table from Lech

Wałęsa, said something about getting everything down on paper 'in black and white'. There was a sudden intake of breath from the audience and everyone began to whisper. I turned to Maria and asked what was happening, why was everyone fussing, had I missed something? Maria said:

- Didn't you hear it? His accent. He is not Polish, his accent betrayed him. It was absolutely not Polish. This communist is a Jew.

- We don't normally get to hear him speak in public at all. This is the first time we have actually heard him. Now we know why.

Later, she talked about this as if something had been made clear, as if Jagielski's accent made a real difference to events, as if this explained something.

Two nights later we were back in the same cinema to look at the rough cut of Wajda's latest film, *Man of Steel*. I had seen Wajda on TV many times, and listened to him talk about his work on *Man of Marble* and *Workers '80*. Here he was at a showing of *Man of Iron*. After the film there was a desultory question and answer session which was equally unsatisfactory for both Wajda and the audience. The questions were polite, deferential, but listless and uninspired I wanted to ask a question, but the two students I had gone with were too shy to translate for me, and I was not confident enough of my Polish to try a question on my own. I thought my opportunity had passed, but when the session was over my companions went off to find the toilets, Wajda was stood in front of the screen watching the audience file out. Taking my courage to the limit I approached him.

He was very charming. I said how much I had enjoyed his films over the years, and that *Man of Marble* had been

a remarkable experience. There was a pause. He could have made his escape there and then. Wajda said:
- But? There is a but. Please go on.
  Your latest film worries me.
- Go on, please.
- I fear you are celebrating a workers' victory too soon. The workers, the union, they are not organising fast enough. They don't have much time, I'm sure. You must have heard the rumours. And here you make a film showing the Party and milicja as a bunch of power-crazy drunkards, where the workers just have to be good guys to win. It's premature. I'm certain. I don't think Solidarność has won anything more than a moral victory. The authorities are much more resilient than you give them credit for. This is just a skirmish compared to what is yet to come...

Wajda nodded his head, shrugged, looked at the last of the audience trailing out of the cinema. I thought I had offended him, that he was about to walk off in a huff. Then he spoke very quietly:
- You may be right. It is not over yet. I sense something is not right tonight. I look at the people who came here. Only students and intellectuals. No workers. Maybe we should be discussing this in Nowa Huta. But anyway these people need some hope. I could not have said to them what you said to me, though I feel you may be right. I could not do it. So what kind of film would you have me make?

I could not answer, but it was one of the few times when I felt like John Reed, part of something, part of the debate, as if I were making a difference, as if I was in the right place at the right time.[11]

---

[11] John Reed, the American author of *Ten Days That Shook the World*, an eye witness account of the crucial moments of the

Burning Worm

*

Dorota, another of my students, came back from visiting her family in Gdańsk. She said that she had gone to the cinema to see *Last Train from Gun Hill*. But as soon as the cinema was full they had locked the doors and shown *Man of Iron* instead. The manager would not unlock the doors after the film until the projectionist had rewound the film and had made good his escape by a couple of minutes. My friend said that one of the locals told her this arrangement had been going on for some months now.

*

This revolution is being fought out in film too. If the opposition have their documentaries and their Wajda, the authorities have their images of order and hierarchy to purvey too. I noticed posters for the film *Zamach Stanu*.[12] They were everywhere - on windows, walls, hoardings, noticeboards. I went to see the film and found that it was about the military coup that brought Marshal Piłsudski to power in 1926, thereby demolishing the unstable infant democracy that followed the first world war to install a reactionary military regime. The film played for months and months, and seemed to visit every cinema in turn. At first there were enthusiastic comments about how Poland was having its history returned to it, that at last Piłsudski could be debated in public. Indeed the film was quite well made, and the subject of Piłsudski had been one of those grey areas that plagued Polish life under the 'communists'. Besides, it was a Polish domestic

Russian Revolution.

[12]*Zamach Stanu* - Coup d'etat.

production, and apart from *A Bridge Too Far* - in which Poles also figured - Poland could not afford to import many foreign films that year. But by September everyone was bored stiff with *Zamach Stanu*. I met one of my students on the main market. He was prowling, growling, discontented. He gestured at a torn poster flapping in the breeze.

- That old thing again, he said contemptuously. Why don't they change it? Everyone in Poland must have seen it two or three times by now.

Looking back I realised that having the film show for so long was not just a financial manoeuvre. It was also part of the preparation for Martial Law.

lucy

Her name was Łucja, but she preferred to be known as Lucy. Lucy used to ride a motorbike when I first met her. She had just come through a divorce from her childhood sweetheart, Andrzej. 'My Andrzej' she used to call him in spite of the divorce.

She was an English teacher at the university. It was a job she hated with a passion, though her students told me she was a very good teacher and that her examination success rate was unequaled. She had a tiny button nose on which her round glasses refused to sit quietly, round eyes set in a round face. She had what she called 'a teepically Poleesh fess'. She never spoke of her father, who had apparently died just after she was born of some injury sustained during the war. She did tell me that her surname - Szatoba - was a corruption derived from the French name Chateau Bas, Low Castle, and thus she claimed descent from one of the French generals who had tramped across Poland to die in Russia for Napoleon and the dream of Revolutionary Liberation. Later I learned that Szatoba was her married name. Her maiden name was the less elegant Dzurkowska; her students sometimes called her Jerk-off. She was also known as Juicy Lucy, though I preferred not to know how she got that nickname.

She lived in a huge crumbling prewar apartment block, and shared the place with the world's largest private collection of wasps. All dead, of course. Dead and pinned and mounted in massive cabinets lining the walls. The flat was cold, gloomy, hideously ugly, but she rented it cheaply because the owner was away - in America or Canada, he had been gone so long nobody could remember which. Lucy had been made responsible for insuring and taking care of the wasps. Everyone assumed that the owner, in spite of the wasp collection, had 'jumped ship' and decided to stay in the West.

Lucy also kept a half share in a small flat that she and her husband had rented when they first married. The housing shortage was such that even after divorce and re-marriage people still had no choice but to inhabit, along with their new partners, the same space they had waited fifteen years to share with their ex-partner. Andrzej was not prepared to give up his share in the flat, and Lucy wanted to retain it, she said, so that she could be near her mother at weekends. Lucy's mother, knew better.

- She only keeps the place so that she can check up on Andrzej's girl friends. She thinks that he won't bring girls home if she is there. I keep telling her, he brings the girls back *because* she's there, but my Lucy is a stubborn, foolish girl. She lives in hope of a reconciliation.

Burning Worm

Her mother was rather deaf and kept her hearing aid turned up as loud as possible. Its high pitched whistle used to drive everyone around her to distraction, but the old lady never seemed to notice.

Lucy would often drop in at my place for tea after work, but once she came hammering on my door late at night. When I opened up she collapsed in tears. Her eyes were red, her face swollen and she was utterly exhausted. After she calmed a little I made tea and she sat hunched over almost double, still in her coat, clutching the hot glass. Earlier in the day she had a hospital appointment. After some tests and a prolonged examination - nearly seven hours - the doctor had told her she had only a short time to live and should therefore make the most of it and go out and enjoy herself.

She pulled a huge crumpled X-Ray picture from her bag and said that she was suffering from a rare and inoperable condition. She tapped the X-ray picture with a damp forefinger.

- My insides are all reversed, she said, sobbing and splashing her tea. You know, the wrong way round. Look, my appendix is over here and it should be there.... She started to cry again.

- When did you start having trouble?

- During divorce. Just stomach trouble, you know. But it didn't go away. So I went to the doctor, but he couldn't help me. And so after a while he sent me to the hospital, and they couldn't do anything. So I ask to see specialist and he said there was nothing. Just nerves, he said. But I knew that wasn't right so I went back, and now he tells me I'm gonna die! I'm gonna die!

- When did you see the specialist?

- Lots of times. Nine, maybe ten times. Why? What does it matter? He's told me truth at last. I'm gonna die!

- But he never said anything about this before, did he?

- He's told me now, that's the important thing. Do you think, will Andrzej come round when he hears about this?

I held the X-ray picture up to the light.

- Why should you die? If all your bits and pieces worked OK up to now, why should you suddenly die? Nothing broke or ruptured or anything. I mean if it was serious you would never have lived to be 32.

- 37.

- What?

- 37. I'm 37... Lucy dabbed her face. I just had small pain, and then he said how everything was all back to front and how I should go out and have a good time before.... why should I die if everything was working up to now.... ? You won't tell anyone will you?

- What?

- About me being 37...

- Look, I said. I turned the X-ray picture over and held it up to the light. Lucy looked at it again. She reached out and took the picture from me.

- Hey, everything is right way round again!

She held the picture out in front of her, turning it back and forth.

- I'm not sure, I said. But I think the shiny side is held towards the viewer.

Lucy wailed.

- Son of a bitch! Oh my God! Oh I feel such a fool.... Oh I'll just die of shame....

- I think you saw the specialist once too often, Lucy. It's his way of telling you to.... well, leave him alone and start enjoying yourself.

- He was drunk. I swear I smelt vodka on his breath. I sue the bastard!

I did not see her again for several weeks.

In spite of her daredevil, long distance, solo motor cycling stunts across the Polish countryside she could not reconcile herself to her divorce. Instead of finding other new ways she persisted in trying to revive the old patterns of her existence, as if by some magic she could make her life again as it had once been. Crushed back on her self she was aware of the limitations of her resources, and for a while strove to find ways to express herself and break out into the world. The motorbike was one of her strategies. But slowly, certainly she became someone for whom the only joy in life resided in finding new ways to make herself miserable. She had pushed herself a long way in this direction by the time we first met. She could not find a way back.

I visited her at the cold flat with the wasps several times, but Lucy invited me to the flat she shared with her ex-husband only once. She served coffee in tall glasses and we sat up to a table decorated with hand embroidered napkins, all prim and proper. It was one of those nights when Andrzej brought a girl back with him. I had never met the man, and rather hoped that he would look into the sitting room just to say hello. But he took a studied disinterest in Lucy. Seeing her coat in the hall he took the girl straight to his bedroom, returning only to search for glasses in the kitchen. I assume he had some vodka, which in a time of Solidarność ordained prohibition was reason in itself for a thirsty girl to go home with him. Lucy listened to Andrzej crashing around in the kitchen and then suddenly started to tell me in detail about an article she had read in a newspaper recently in which it was said that there were certain knives, made from a certain kind of steel, that destroyed the vitamin content of vegetables upon contact. Abruptly she dropped the business with the knives and said that Andrzej had just bought a new pair of expensive Austrian skis for hard currency.

- You know he's thinking of joining the Party? My Andrzej, the wriggling little worm! In the Party! I can hardly believe it. When he told me I thought it was start of some joke. But no, he's serious.... It's only a career move he says, nothing more, but of course he will lose all his friends, nobody will speak to him. And anyway what will he do there? He is politically illiterate. He just wants the perks: medical privileges, fillings for his teeth, the private shops, Party ski resorts - and whisky for his girl friends....

Lucy began to tell me about her attempt to escape from Poland, two years previously. She was divorced by than and had an English boy friend she had met through a language teaching course. His name was Trevor. Lucy's mother liked Trevor - the first and only one of Lucy's boyfriends who met her approval - and had nicknamed him Polish style as 'Trevorek', Little Trevor, though sometimes she called him 'Worek', which was her private joke: Worek means sack in Polish.

Lucy had organised a scholarship for herself in London, and after months of negotiating and waiting in offices for signatures on documents she had finally got everything she needed for her departure. In theory she would return to Poland when the scholarship was up, but it was easy to see through the ruse. She hoped her boyfriend would offer her marriage when she arrived in London. At least a marriage of convenience. It was as transparent as that, but she had obtained her passport and permission to go to London, and it is possible that the Security Services really were not keeping an eye on her after all. Still, she was clumsy. She put an advertisement in the newspaper to sell her skis, she sold all her furniture - which was why she now rented the furnished apartment with the wasps. But even though she had the flat with the wasps and half of the flat with Andrzej, she confined herself to the back room at her mother's apartment, living on a diet of tea, apples and white cheese to save money in order to buy all the black market dollars she could lay her hands on. It was, she explained, a matter of subterfuge.

And then she had a going away party.

I'm still not sure that the milicja had her spotted. She traveled by train to Gdynia, and hauled her luggage aboard the boat for London. The milicja made no attempt to stop her. They let the boat leave port, they let the boat get out into the Baltic. And Lucy began to believe that she had got away with it. Unfortunately, just as they were about to quit Polish territorial waters, the woman with whom she shared the cabin peeped inside the unlocked suitcase Lucy had left on her bunk. The woman took one look at the fat piles of dollars and pounds and reported it to the ship's Captain, who radioed the coastal patrol. The ship heaved-to, a milicja launch pulled alongside to take Lucy back to port.

A People's Court confiscated her passport and all her foreign currency and fined her a quarter of her salary for the next two years, not because she intended to leave the country, but because of her currency offence. Rather than spend her black market currency in the government's Dollars-only store, she had tried to smuggle her black market currency, currency that had once been smuggled into the country, back out of the country. Ignoring the fact that the government had made the black market semi-legal by creating Dollars-only shops precisely to relieve the population of their black market cash, the judge explained that Lucy was guilty of speculating at the expense of the state.

She told me this while we drank coffee - an incredible luxury for her - and the sequence of events certainly explained her poverty and despair.

Lucy finished her story. I gave my hand embroidered, folk art table napkin a close examination and tried to think of something to say. I could hear Andrzej and his girl friend grunting and thrashing on the other side of the wall. I looked up to see Lucy spooning black coffee grains from the bottom of her glass into her mouth. She was chewing the coffee grounds furiously. A tear ran down her face.

- I hate to see anything wasted, she said. Anything at all.

snowman

Trzemesznia, another of our teaching centres a few miles from Kraków, was a typical Polish village, spread along a mile and a half of winding hilly roadside. From the top of the valley, where the houses faded imperceptibly into the next ribbon of village, it was possible on a clear day to see the peaks of the distant Carpathian mountains as they breasted the clouds.

Once Maria suggested that we should go for a walk up the valley. It was a good idea. With both teaching and administrative duties there were some days when I simply did not get out of the building at all. It was already dark when we set out, but the moon was well up and the road glittered as if encrusted with tiny gems. The night was clear. We walked briskly up the valley, past the log road bridge, past the waterfall frozen to a thousand shades of green, past the roadside shrines to the Virgin Mary - decorated now with plastic bouquets made brittle by the cold. Above us the stars gleamed clean and malicious through the mist of our breath.

Maria assured me:

- There is only one road through the valley. It's not possible to get lost.

So we walked on, much further up the valley than I had ever been before. Eventually we came to a partly constructed house by the roadside. It had a steeply raked roof, a porch, a well protected south facing ground floor balcony, and it was set in its own grounds. Tools and building materials lay scattered about the place as if they had been dropped the moment the clock struck five, there was a high barbed wire fence around the site, and a guard dog on a long leash growled from the shadows. It was clear that this was to be a grand private villa.

An old couple trudged past us. The man carried a huge bundle of sticks on a frame strapped to his back. The woman was bandy legged, dressed in black and had a shawl wrapped tightly about her head and face. She carried two pails on a yoke over her shoulders. She noticed us looking at the villa. Her husband walked on past us, but she stopped and turned to speak:

- A bloody scandal, don't you think? A bloody scandal. And there's fine people, people like yourself I'm sure, even if you are from Kraków to judge by the fashion of your clothes, fine people I'm sure just the same, waiting to get a place of their own. Fifteen years they wait, some of them. And there's them bastards…

She gestured at the house, hawked and spat. Her
husband waited quietly a few paces away looking at
nothing in particular.

- What does he want with another place? Eh? Sixteen I
heard on the news he's got. Sixteen villas. And you sir,
and your fine lady, I ask you, how many houses is it
possible for a person to live in at the one and same time.
One is enough for poor folk, and I don't suppose it's any
different for you neither. Even if you do come all the way
from Kraków, and folks do say that people from there is
not like us. Unless you ain't human then one home is
enough and any more is a sin.

There was a moment's silence. Maria and I looked at
the villa. The dog had stopped growling and was
whimpering to itself.

Maria said:

- Whose place is it then?

The old lady took a step closer.

- Szczepański,that bastard Government Minister what's
supposed to run the telly and the radio and such forth.[13]
And he's got some black whores to install when the

---

[13]Maciej Szczepański, Chairman of the State Committee for
Radio and Television. In October 1981 the Party Plenum
dismissed Szczepański from his post and accused him of
various offences: he was to be tried for misusing budget
resources, embezzling 2,900,000 złoties at a time when Polish
TV could not even afford film for cameras. Later it was
revealed that although he earned 284,000 złoties per year, he
had used his position on the Central Committee to buy seven
private cars, a helicopter, two executive jets, a yacht, a farm,
several villas, a 16-room mini palace, an enormous collection
of pornographic films, and a 'villa' in Kenya; he also ran a
string of four black prostitutes, maintained two black
mistresses and had bank accounts in Switzerland and London.

moment is right. I seen 'em. He brought 'em here one day. Prancing and a-primping they was with their bosoms all undone.

The husband shifted uneasily under his burden.

- Arrested he should be, for living off proletarian labours and such like..... And for doing it with blacks too, I shouldn't wonder. Not that the likes of us cares mind you, for even though we grow the food they eat, we are the enemies of the people, according to the newspapers.

Maria made as if to walk on. I said good-bye to the old lady but she, looking at Maria said to me:

- Have you got her belly up yet young man? She's a pretty one and if you don't there's others will do it for you. Make babies! That's what youth is for. Make babies! There's nothing else in the world, you mark my words.

Maria gave a yelp and skittered up the road her heels searching frantically for traction on the ice. The old lady took a step closer, laughing.

- Oh my, there's a goose if ever I saw one.... Youth! Youth! It's wasted on the young.

We bade each other a cheery good night and eventually I managed to catch up with Maria.

After a few minutes of walking in silence Maria said:

- There's a cafe up ahead. We can stop for a drink if you'd like.

And sure enough, as we rounded the bend the great black bulk of a public building loomed at us. We passed a huge column of snow, climbed the steps, knocked the slush off our boots and stepped inside. We were almost overwhelmed by the dense fug of smoke, coke fumes and unwashed bodies. There was a sudden silence as every head in the place turned to inspect us. There was tension in the air. The faces were not friendly. A small round character stepped up to us, a gold tooth gleaming in the centre of his upper jaw. In his lapel he had a large enameled pin that said Society of Friends of the Soviet Union.

He shook us warmly by the hand.

- So you've come at last.... welcome, Comrades.

- Er.... were you expecting us?

- But of course. We hoped you might be here before dark, but.... you're here now, so what's the difference? Eh?

- We were just out for a walk...

- But you're the people from Kraków, right? Here to see the snowman?

- Snowman?

- We were just walking...

- This snowman, it's a model of Lenin...

I think he read doubt in our faces.

- Didn't you see it on the way in comrade?

He opened the door and stepped outside. He pointed at the pile of snow. From behind us there was a chorus of curses and complaints about the draught.

- The Socialist Pioneers of Youth spent all day on it. I phoned the papers at lunch time. They should have been here by now, unless of course, they've been nobbled by Solidarność.

- Lenin? I said.

Maria pulled at my arm.

- Well, all right, so the sun melted it a bit, but you should have been here earlier.

Neither Maria nor I spoke. He clattered down the steps saying loudly.

- I'll have to write a report on this. It sounds like sabotage to me...

Maria said:

- Oh my gosh just look at the time, I didn't realise it was so late, we have to get back, must dash, it's been so nice and we don't even have time for a glass of tea'.

The friend of the Soviet Union stood watching us as we backed away down the path and round the column of snow.

From the darkened road we could hear him calling:

- The image of Lenin, it was. Beard and all. Ask anybody, they'll tell you.

We retraced our steps down the valley. A wind had sprung up and the sky was clouding over rapidly. As we passed the partly built villa the first snow flakes began to swirl about us. We had taken our exercise just in time. Tomorrow it would not be possible to walk at all.

delivery

Poland is poor. It is grey and dull and dirty. But you don't go there to look at the scenery. In Poland the joke is that things are so bad even the shortages are rationed, but then most of the planned shortages also go unfilled. Some joke. When I first visited Poland in the mid 1970s a packet of coffee cost half a month's salary. There were no biros. A plastic washing up bowl was a status item. Denims were never casual. Beards were compulsory. Tampons were items from science fiction. Poland's diseases - tuberculosis, hepatitis, cholera - are all diseases of poverty. Only once did I manage to buy a fruit that was not an apple. I bought a grapefruit. It was several days before I could bring myself to touch it. The fleshy golden orb sat on my windowsill until my conscience would give me no peace and I called my neighbours in to help me eat it. But that was in 1975. By 1981 oranges were a subject of almost erotic fantasy.

*

Ramondo loved children. When he returned from Seville he brought with him a large bag of oranges for his neighbours' kid. I was there when he presented his gift to seven year old Piotrek. Piotrek took an orange and was obviously delighted with it. Then, turning on his heel, Piotrek raised his arm and hurled the orange at the floor with all his might. The orange burst into pulp and a spurt of juice. Piotrek's face cracked and he started to wail: 'The ball's no good! It doesn't bounce.' After drying his eyes Piotrek's parents, sat down, explained that it was not a ball, and to his amazement showed him how to peel and eat an orange.

When we left the house, Ramondo and I stood looking up at the clear winter sky. The same stars that twinkled above us were twinkling above the west too. Ramondo said maybe it had been a mistake to take oranges. He did not think the parents would eat them. They would save them for the child. And perhaps it was wrong to give the kid a taste for something he might never again see. Ramondo was in torment. His gift had turned out to be a complex problem. I said maybe Piotrek would think of it as a magic moment, a bright spot in a bleak year. Ramondo replied that in Poland you could never do right for doing wrong. Perhaps by making a gift you were propping up the regime that had made the mess in the first place. But how could anyone who had it in their power to make a gift, not make that gift? Really, I am from Seville, I had to give them oranges.

I too would have loved a slice of orange, only a slice, but my hunger for fresh fruit is only a few months old.

*

One observer calculated that Poles spent an average of seven hours a day standing in queues, with temperatures well below freezing. In my office at the university a message was waiting for me from The British Council in Warsaw advising employees what to do should the Soviets invade. The message read:

> If an emergency should become apparent you are to make your way immediately to Warsaw, where the British Council and the Embassy will prepare to receive you. The Embassy staff have agreed that an RAF Hercules transport will fly in and take all British nationals out. British Council employees in Gdańsk and Gdynia should seek passage on any friendly ship in port. These instructions apply to all employees except those resident in Kraków, which will almost certainly be cut off immediately. It is deemed unsafe for these employees to attempt the journey to Warsaw. They are advised to fill their bath with water, stock up their cupboard with food and stay off the streets while hostilities last.

Fill the cupboard with food? Where have these people been living for the last six months. Do they think Poland is like the embassy shop? There is no food. And the water supply is as erratic as the electricity. And do they seriously think the Soviets will let the RAF fly into a battle zone? Bloody, bloody, bloody idiots.

*

There was a rumour that a stall on the market had a delivery of dates. On the strength of the rumour we had been queuing for several hours. I had been there since just after 2.00 and I was not among the first-comers. It was about 6.30 in the evening when the stall opened and the line began to move. It was dark, It was misty. Fresh flurries of snow lay on our shoulders and heads. I think I must have been about number 200 in the line. We could not see the head of the queue, but with the first customers there came angry shouts drifting back through the mist. Slowly an old man in a fur cap, leaning heavily on a stick, limped towards us.

- Sons of bitches!' he yelled, brandishing a small brown paper bag. 'Sons of bitches! I fuck you all! I fuck you! D'you hear me?

He waved the bag at the queue.

- Dates? Did they tell you it was dates? Well it's plums. Filthy, shitty, dried up, smoked plums like you can get anywhere.

He hurled the bag to the ground and the plums made dark smudges in the snow.

- Did I do something? Am I a criminal? Am I a person anymore?

He struggles with his coat and finally dragged out his identity card and a whole wad of papers.

- Look here! It says citizen. So? What does that mean? I'll tell you what it means. It means they think I'm a simpleton. It means they can abuse me, they can do just as they please....

On and on he went. A few people, realising that there were no dates to be had, moved away, pretending for sanity's sake that they had not really been taken in by the cruel fiction. But the old man stayed put.

- Very well then. If they want me to be a nothing, a zed, a zombie, a robot, I'll do it. Let's put an end to this stupid game once and for all. I resign. I resign from Poland. I resign from being a citizen. I resign from being human. I'm no longer a person. I'm a thing. I resign.

He threw the fist full of papers, his ration tickets, his pension book, his identity card, all of them, onto the ground. He turned his back and stalked off. The limping figure was soon swallowed by the dark and mist.

We stared after him like sheep. He had left us a problem. We did not know how to react. Was he serious? He could not live without his papers, could not eat without his ration tickets. He would soon be in trouble with the milicja. In fact, if there were any milicja listening to him, then he was already in trouble. How could we help him? Pretend we had not heard, not seen. Pretend we knew nothing about it. It would not be possible for us to return his papers to him without compromising ourselves. Would the milicja accuse us of having antisocial contacts? If we gave the papers to the milicja would they suspect us of stealing them, of mugging the old man, of using them to forge food stamps, of being connected with the black market? And how could we return the papers to the old man without forcing him to face up to the whole damned mess once more? Who had the heart to that? It was easier to do nothing.

Burning Worm

A tiny, stooped woman in black stepped forward from the line, bent and gathered the papers, then moved on a little and gathered the plums one by one, feeling for them under the fresh snow with her fingers. She put the plums back in the bag, and then, holding both bag and papers aloft for all to see, she set off into the mist shouting:

- Excuse me, sir! Excuse me! I think you dropped something...

In a moment she was gone, swallowed in the gloom. I think she shamed us all with that simple action.

*

Night after night. Just as I'm falling asleep it starts. Suddenly I'm whooping and wheezing and gasping for breath, punching myself to get air into my lungs. After an hour or so the asthma usually subsides. The sweat on my face and body dries. I wash, rearrange the bedclothes. I lie down, switch out the light. It starts again. One night, just like this. I could not sleep. Sometimes I go out onto the balcony and start my deep breathing exercises.... In two three, out two three, in two three...

It must have been about three in the morning. My breath wheezed and crackled in the freezing air. I looked down from my balcony onto the railway line. The neon lights of the local station flickered into life. A few moments later the earth trembled and a huge military train rolled into sight. I counted over fifty wagons and trucks, thirty two of them were flatcars with tanks, armoured cars, amphibious transport, jeeps, communications tenders and lorries. In spite of the cold soldiers sat with their legs dangling from the edge of the cars, peering into the dark, breathing clouds of frosted breath. The train jangled, clattered and screeched to a halt. After a few seconds the brakes whined and the train moved on again. The balcony vibrated under my feet.

I left my flat at around 6.30 that morning. I had been woken by the noise of trains in the nearby rail yard and had been unable to get back to sleep. I felt a morning walk might clear my head, and hoped a few stalls at the market would be open early. I might be able to buy a chicken. The temperature was about minus 15 degrees and there was a drifting fog. Breath rasped in my chest.

I walked along the railway embankment and then cut through the estate to the huge expanse of wasteland that served as a local marketplace. I wandered onto the wasteland with its clumps of frosted grass and frozen puddles. Visibility was poor, but as the fog shifted I saw a queue of people. I admit it was a small queue, only about ten people, but there was no mistaking it. It had the air of organisation, resignation and anticipation that hover over a serious queue. The odd thing was that there was no kiosk or stall visible, indeed the nearest building was over 220 yards distant. This was a queue in the middle of nowhere. It was almost a metaphysical joke and I wondered if it were not some piece of Polish experimental theatre in the making.

I stopped to look, all thought of a market chicken gone. Whatever and whoever they were, they clearly knew something I did not. I asked what the line was for, and one man said:
- A delivery is expected.
- A delivery of what? I asked.

Everyone shrugged. As I tagged on to the end of the line I could make out the vague shapes of people moving in our direction from distant corners of the estate to join the queue. Nobody spoke. I found myself rewriting a poem in my head:

> Dear Roger
> There's a housewife
> In a queue
> Wondering what the
> Bloody hell
> She's gonna do[14]

After about ten minutes a lorry pulled up and noisily deposited a huge steel container at the head of the queue. A woman with an enormous key trudged past us to the container and unlocked it. She swung open the doors. From floor to ceiling the container was packed with boxes of washing powder.

- 40 złoties apiece, she said and started trading.

This was the first washing powder we had seen for nearly seven months.

It was my turn at the front of the line. I asked for four packets. The woman handed them over.

- One for mommy, one for granny, one for sister, and one for the bachelor himself.

I dropped the plan to buy a chicken, and set off immediately to give Maria a packet of the precious powder.

I took a route that I did not normally walk, behind the barracks. The fog was lifting and the air was warming slightly. When I reached the area by the barracks it was a sea of churned, frozen mud, and parked on the mud were

---

[14]Roger McGough [b.1937], Liverpool poet, author of: 'Nun standing in a queue, wondering what it would be like to buy fish and chips for two.' *The Mersey Sound*, Penguin, 1967.

about forty squat dull green tanks. Over by the railway line a series of flat cars were parked and a group of soldiers were slowly manoeuvring a tank onto a ramp. I did not slow my pace, judged it unwise to loiter or ask questions.

By a ragged loop of streets I eventually reached Maria's house, and all the while I walked I could not help wondering why there were tanks parked only a few hundred yards from my house. Had they been delivered to the paratroopers? Why? Paratroopers do not usually have tanks.

*

Maria let me into the flat and ushered me into the kitchen, then went out to make sure her parents were not around. She was clearly very excited about something, She came back into the kitchen on tiptoe.

- Listen. My father has just returned from a top Party meeting down in Krynica. Albin Siwak[15] was there to give them all a pep-talk and he said that there were special plans. The army will stage a coup and all the Solidarność leaders will be arrested. Things will be bad for a while, perhaps very bad, but then everything will be all OK.

---

[15] Albin Siwak. Noted Party boor, anti-Semite and trade union activist. The Extraordinary Ninth Communist Party Congress, July 1981, delegated him to represent the Warsaw Party organisation and elevated him to the Central Committee and the Politburo. His inclusion in the top ranks of the Party at this stage doomed the Party's efforts to reform itself. The magazine *Fermentacje*, published by Siwak's trade union organisation, printed sections of the anti-Semitic tract *Protocols of the Elders of Zion* throughout 1981.

The idea clearly pleased her enormously. She smiled as she spoke and twirled about, which was most unlike her. Siwak was a top Party man, on the Central Committee. Maria was pleased. She had found something in life that made sense. It made sense to me too. I felt for the first time in months that I knew what was going on, that I had located the hidden curriculum of daily life, I too could relax a little. If I agreed or disagreed, it made no difference. Someone, somewhere was in charge, something was going to happen. But a coup.... I began to think about the tanks parked near my house. I said:

- That will be the end of Solidarność, the reforms.... everything.

Maria shrugged.

- Whatever. It didn't work fast enough. We can't sustain this level of chaos much longer.

*

But what can I say normal categories of life and thought do not seem to apply here. How can a highly cultured, highly regimented, industrialised state have got into such a mess? Western governments have given money to a stupid, callous, careless regime. Western governments believed the regime's propaganda. They encouraged it. Yet the fact is that we have a Third World state right here in Europe.

blind man & rats

In February 1981 the British Council send me off to the tiny hamlet of Stegna on the Baltic coast. I am to teach on an intensive refresher course for Polish teachers of English. Travelling by train it is normally a six hour journey, from Kraków to Warsaw. And then another six hours from Warsaw to Gdańsk. But with the shortages and strikes, a number of trains have been canceled. Those that are running are so crowded that a reservation is just a complicated and rather unfunny joke. I suspect many passengers no longer even bother to buy a ticket in the hope that the conductor will not be able to penetrate the densely packed corridors. I am right. When the train pulls into the station it is packed so tight passengers cannot get along the corridor to get on or off. There is a vicious rugby scrum of passengers at the doors, trying to get onto the train. So arrivals wishing to leave the train throw their luggage out of the window and then climb after it.

I end up jammed upright with a party of soldiers. Khaki sardines. As soon as they realise I speak English they drag out a bottle of vodka and all, in turn, solemnly toast the Anglo-Polish alliance of 1939. After half an hour we are pleasantly smashed, and it is still only about seven the morning. Suddenly a conductress squeezes through the throng to check tickets. She sees the vodka bottle circulating, lets out a yelp and disappears. A couple of minutes later an officer appears. He gives the soldiers a dressing down on the subject of how to behave in front of foreigners, and adds a little warning about the dangers of sentiment invested in ancient and irrelevant alliances. Glassy eyed, the soldiers straightened their ties and mumbled: Yes sir, thank you sir, and saluted as best they could in the crush. The officer glared at me, and then disappeared. After a few embarrassed moments one of the soldiers winked.

- Bastards, officers, no?

- Hey, why don't we teach him how to sleep standing up?

So they did. The train, now running several hours late, eventually emptied out a little and I found a seat. The man sitting opposite me was wearing a TKN[16] badge signifying that he was a teacher for the Flying University. A year ago this had been an illegal subversive organisation, harassed by the milicja. Now they wore badges. He had an enormous Piłsudski/Wałęsa mustache and he was reading a volume by Solzhenitsyn, holding it so that everyone in the compartment could see the cover. He looked up and caught my eye

- And what does sir think of our country?
- Pretty. Very Pretty.

He nodded, smiled and looked out of the window, as if to say, can this really be called pretty? My eyes are sore, my knees and feet are swollen from standing, my back feels as if someone has driven nails into my spine and my mouth tastes like a rat had a nasty intestinal event in it. Does this man from TKN want to talk to me? I hope not. I want to sleep I am desperate to sleep. After a minute he said:

- You know we are number eleven in the world league of industrial nations. Poles invented Vitamins and Esperanto. A Pole collaborated with Einstein. And now look at us. We are a kind of Cargo cult, forever waiting for the good life to drop from the skies. Other nations live in civilisation: we live in drama.

---

[16]TKN: Towarzystwo Kursow Nauk: Society for Academic Courses, known as The Flying University. Based on an academic society established in 1885 in Russian occupied Poland, dedicated to preserving Polish national identity through uncensored education in the Polish language. Founded January 1978 by scholars, writers and teachers, challenging the Party monopoly on education and research outlets.

He looked out of the window for a moment then turned back to his book.

Our train was held up. We sat in a siding for hours picking our noses, counting corn stooks, rattling newspapers, going to the lavatory out of boredom, listening to metal cool. Eventually another train pulled in alongside us. It was a Soviet military train with armoured vehicles shrouded in canvas loaded on flat cars. Further along there was a cattle truck. The doors of the truck swung open and soldiers dangled their legs.

There is a rumour circulating that a Polish border guard has been shot dead by the Russians. The story goes that a train stopped at the border check point, but was stormed by angry peasants who thought it contained food being shipped to the Soviet Union. The train was standing in Poland but when the Russians saw it was being opened up they fired into the crowd, killing a border guard who was trying to control the mob. Polish soldiers fired back and killed a Russian. When the peasants got into the wagons they did not find food, but dozens and dozens of Polish milicja uniforms.

On the flat car opposite me an Asiatic soldier as big as a jockey, yellow and miserable, and carrying a rifle and bayonet almost as tall as he was, pulled his collar up and his fur hat down. He was guarding a huge armoured vehicle covered by tarpaulin. The Poles watched him for a few minutes then they could stand it no longer. A window slid open and a voice shouted, in Russian.

- Hey comrade, you want change money? Eh? Money change?

The soldier's face remained blank. Other windows opened:

- Hey comrade, comrade…

The soldier slowly turned his back and began to shuffle his feet. The insults began to flow.

- Want to buy a wrist watch? Ticky-tock, Comrade?

Finally an officer jumped out of a cattle truck and walked down the train to investigate the racket. He ordered the soldier to stand on the other side of the canvas covered vehicle, away from the Poles. The soldier moved out of sight. A voice said:

- Perhaps the comrade general would like to change money.

The officer turned and began to walk away.

- What's this? Retreat and wait for winter.

The train dissolved into hooting, and jeering. The officer returned along the track, his hand resting on his pistol, his boots crunching the ballast.

- I hope you freeze your nuts off!

With a gesture of his wrist the officer ordered the door of the cattle truck closed. Our carriage settled down to wait again, but this time the silence was broken by the occasional chuckle.

*

What seems like days later, after a nightmare change of trains in Warsaw, my train pulled into Gdańsk. Opposite the main platform a team of men were at work with buckets of white paint and brushes on long poles. They were writing in letters ten feet high, the words: *Solidarność i Wolność.*[17]

The village of Stegna was pleasant enough, a few houses, a half timbered church with the second largest painted ceiling in Europe as the parish priest informed me.

---

[17]Solidarity and Freedom.

There had at one time been a small fishing fleet operating out of Stegna, but that had been before the war when the village had been part of Germany and was known as Steegen. Fishing has finished in these parts now. Pollution of the Polish stretch of the Baltic coast has killed off large numbers of fish, so it is not economic to retain the fleet. The boats are hauled up on the beach where they moulder away quietly beside the rotting fish.

We were working in a small residential centre. The place was a holiday centre for sports enthusiasts, so it was well equipped, and the food was very good. Huge bowls of steaming soup. Small pieces of dusty chocolate followed every meal. Next door to us there was a huge Marine barrack.

On our sixth or seventh night in Stegna there was a power cut. It came without warning, not even a flickering of the lamps.

I was already jittery. That day the guard on the Marine barrack had been doubled and armed patrols with steel helmets, fixed bayonets and backpacks moved along the perimeter, through the woods, along the beaches and also through the village. The officers were very tense. It was clear that something was about to happen, but nobody knew what.

The night was so dark - there was no moon - that when the lights went out my first thought was that I had suddenly gone blind. There was not a glimmer of light anywhere. I got out of bed and groped my way to the window, but I could not make out a star or even a vague skyline. There was no discernible difference between the darkness of my room and that which lay outside. The Marine barracks, where the soldiers often stayed up late singing, and where the main gate and duty officer's hut were usually to be seen through the trees was absolutely invisible.

I did not believe a night could be so black. I was sure I had been struck down by some peculiar nervous disease, my blindness was almost a fact. Fighting down my panic I groped my way to the corridor thinking that someone somewhere must be moving about with a torch or a candle or a box of matches - though matches were almost a black market commodity by this time. But no. All was silent, all was dark.

I fumbled my way back to bed and tried not to list the diseases which might lead to sudden blindness. I had run out of symptoms when the lights came back on. I very nearly wet myself for joy. I was utterly exhausted and fell asleep immediately.

Next morning when I went down to breakfast there were a dozen heavily armed Marines standing around with fixed bayonets. They eyed us very suspiciously and when we asked why they were here they just grunted:

- Carry on as usual.

During breakfast I watched a party of Marines under an officer covering over our entire building with a huge camouflage netting in which branches had been twined. Still nobody explained what was going on.

I had free time around 11.00 that morning and decided to go for a run along the beach to do my exercises. It was an unusually warm day with very little wind and the sea was calm. I ran my usual route: first down to the village. There were armed guards on the post office and at the front of the village alcohol store, which was in any case shut. A notice on the door said that there would be no business done that day. One of the villagers said it had been there since the previous August. I ran through the woods, past another armed patrol, past a platoon of soldiers digging trenches. On the beach there were pairs of Marines stationed every dozen or so yards, right off into the distance. It was very odd. I jogged along in my karate suit and nobody said a word. Eventually I stopped running, found a level stretch of sand and did my exercises. The Marines watched with a kind of disinterested amusement. When I had finished I waved to them and jogged back the way I had come. At the end of the beach there was a watch tower - a Marine watched me through binoculars. I waved at him too.

When I got back to the holiday centre they had some news. Overnight there had been some sort of change of government. Nobody was too clear about what had happened, but one of the officers explained:

- As of this morning the Eighth Plenum of the Central Committee of the Party accepted General Jaruzelski as Prime Minister.

- Who?

- Who's he?

- Minister of Defence, you moron.

It was clear that First Secretary Kania was out, and General Jaruzelski had taken over. Somebody said:

- But I thought Kania had the support of the military...

- Obviously not any more.

- What does it mean to have a General at the top?

- Is it a military coup?

- What does it mean?

A soldier said:

- I think he might be blind. He wears dark glasses, you know? The Russians tortured him when he was in the resistance...

- Yeah, I've seen him. He looks like a worm in dark glasses.

There was sudden silence.

I wondered why the military had been on the alert for this event. Did they really think Poles would rise up at this news? Nobody knew what it meant and it was impossible to assess the importance of such a change. It all seemed important but without context. Everything seemed utterly random.

General Jaruzelski wielded enormous power after his elevation. At the time I thought that talk of a 'military takeover' was exaggerated, and I tried to think of it merely as a cabinet reshuffle. But later I came to think that it was, in fact, not far short of a military takeover. People saw it as an anti-Solidarnosc move, but it seemed more likely that it was intended to take control of internal and external communications, and try to rein in the renegade elements among security services. By this time at least a part of the security service was operating under Soviet control and involved in various acts of provocation. That point seemed to have gone unnoticed in the panic.

But still you could read the event several ways: stave off western aid and interference while negotiating reforms with Solidarność. Stave off Soviet invasion by crushing Solidarność with inertia, starvation, depression. On the other hand Solidarność had no option but to force the government's hand. The union was reluctantly facing up to the fact that if the Party was as incapable as it appeared, the union itself would eventually have to take the lead. That meant going into politics and government for itself. And that meant not only negotiating directly with the Soviets, but clearing up the mess the government and the Party left behind. Not an attractive prospect simply because any dealings with the Soviets would be deemed treachery, and in clearing up the mess the union would soon become as unpopular as the Party.

Before Jaruzelski took over, the Party was backsliding at every opportunity, attempting to slip out of every deal. But Jaruzelski, although a Party member and a senior member of the politburo, is not after confrontation with the union. He seems to support *Odnowa*.[18] Jaruzelski's job may be to protect Poland while the government and the union came to an accommodation. Perhaps that is just wishful thinking. Now, at this minute, who can say for sure?

*

Blind man
Where are you
Leading us
Are you
Leading us?

*

I was away from my flat in Kraków, teaching on intensive courses in the nearby towns and villages, for much of the time. The courses generally lasted 10 days, and I calculate that between November 1980 and March 1981 I did nine courses. I was absent from my flat for 90 days. That is, three months out of five if the days were all added together. Inevitably this caused problems. I had no social life or friends and no time to make them either. I often returned to Kraków at the weekend when the shops were

---

[18]*Odnowa* - renewal.

shut so that I could not buy even the tiny amount of food that was available.

There were other problems too. My timetable was well known in advance and I can only assume that the authorities availed themselves of this information. In March 1981 I returned home from yet another intensive course, and I don't know why, but right from the moment I put my key into the lock I felt that something was wrong. The key felt strange in the lock, the air smelt different. I could not work out what it was, but something was different. It was something small, minute even. Then I saw it. I always put chairs against the wall to leave as large a central space as possible. The chairs in the flat were now half an inch from the wall. Somebody had been in my flat.

I went to Warsaw to collect books and teaching materials, and while I was there I went to the British Council and tried to tell them. The Language Officer listened politely with raised eyebrows and than said:

- Are you sure?

- Absolutely certain.

- Well what have you been doing?

- Nothing. I'm away on courses mostly. Out in the countryside. I don't have time to do anything.

- Well I only ask because one of our teachers was sent home a while ago for dealing in drugs. He had some sort of…. erm…. connection with lorry drivers carrying Heroine up from Turkey. Apparently the Poles discovered he was banking far more than he was earning. I just thought that maybe you…

- No. Nothing.

- Well don't worry about it.

That was all he had to say on the subject.

Burning Worm

*

I stood in a queue at the railway station to buy a ticket back to Kraków. I waited three hours. The woman in front of me was a bent old lady, a tiny widow dressed completely in black. She chatted to me from time to time, but I could not understand a word she said. She had no teeth and so I stood no chance of distinguishing the various kinds of sibilants that Polish specialises in. The fact that I just nodded and said 'Yes, yes' to everything did not worry her. And by the time we neared the head of the queue we had established a good rapport: I kept her place while she visited the bathroom and then she did the same for me.

The ticket office consisted of a series of windows. Usually there are little holes cut in the windows so that the customers can make their wishes known to the sales people, but in this particular office there were no holes, no convenient apertures for doing business. Instead you had to bellow your lungs out in the hope that the person sitting behind the glass, sipping tea and gossiping would hear you, take pity on your plight, see their way clear to doing the job they were paid for and give you a ticket, preferably to your stated destination. Above each window is a small sign saying that this window will be closed for a coffee break at particular times: it is a fine calculation - do you wait when the shutters come down for the break, or do you wander off and join the weary tail end of another queue.

We both saw that the time of the break for this window was approaching, but we decided that after three hours of waiting patiently it would be folly to give up our place: we could wait another 15 minutes, or even half an hour.

Finally the queue moved forward and the widow waddled to the window. On tiptoes she put her head above the polished wooden surface of the bench and peered up at the man behind the window. She said:

- Urffle urffle urffle flurf flur effle.

The man looked down at her with a kind of disdain.

- What's that?

She repeated herself.

- Madam, I can hardly understand a word. Do you wish to buy a train? Or a ticket?

- Urffle.

- Trains? Next window.

And he slammed down the shutter before the widow could say another word. Resigned, she picked up her bags and without a word, without a backward glance, waddled to the end of the next queue. For her another three hour wait. At least I would only have to wait half an hour before the shutter was raised again. Then it would be my turn to bellow at the glass.

A couple of days later I was leaving on yet another intensive course, but this time, before I left I waxed the hall floor. Instead of buffing the floor to a shine, I left the wax. When I returned ten days later the hallway was covered in footprints. I could make out that at least two men had been in the apartment. But what surprised me most were the prints of a large dog. This time they had been very thorough. They had taken the electric sockets from the walls, but in replacing them had left little piles of telltale plaster along the skirting board. Thorough, but careless.

Burning Worm

*

Although officially the Polish army did not go into the villages until the autumn of 1981, in fact they were already a presence as early as March - a full nine months before martial law was declared. Almost immediately after Kania's fall and General Jaruzelski's elevation to Prime Minister in February 1981, military patrols - sometimes several men and an officer, sometimes an armoured vehicle, sometimes just an officer - began to appear in the villages. There was an announcement on the TV which said that the army would be checking up on bottlenecks in the food supply system in order to cut down on the queues that were paralysing the streets and shops and which were draining factories and offices of their productive power.

I remember standing in a village bread queue listening to the manageress explaining to a polite and elegant paratrooper captain that her shop had been closed for the two previous days because the chairman of the local cooperative had not delivered any foodstuffs for her to sell. There had been no delivery of bread from the bakery because they had received no flour from the mill, and the mill had received no grain from the local farmer's cooperative.

- Why should I open up the shop when there is nothing on the shelves. You want me to sit here all day just to remind people what a real shop was like? A simple notice in the window will suffice, she said.

The captain stood in the middle of the bare wooden floor, listened patiently, his head on one side and when she had finished he said:

- In future you will open at the specified times - whether or not you have anything to sell. The state does not pay you to decide when you will open and when you will close. The shop is not here for your convenience, but for the convenience of others. The state pays you to open the shop, so open it. If there has been no delivery you must stand here and say this to your customers. Let them know where the blame lies.

He was quiet but firm. The manageress, who was clearly a powerful figure in the village hierarchy, stammered and blushed to the roots of her hair. Nobody spoke to her in this way.

The people in the queue found themselves mightily entertained: behind the officer's back an old man wagged his finger at the manageress, as if admonishing a child, and a woman tut-tutted. The lieutenant suddenly turned on the queue.

- You are not children and I am not a teacher. If you have anything to say about food supplies in this village, now is the time to say it...

The villagers shuffled their feet. Suddenly everyone was terribly interested in the splintered wooden floor, the vile green paint work, the chipped enamel stove. One or two looked uneasily at the manageress.

- Not with her listening, said one.

The officer eyed them coolly. He knew. He was probably a village boy himself.

- Right, so now we will go and speak with the chairman of the farmers' cooperative that failed to deliver supplies of grain.

The shop emptied and we all followed the captain, splashing through the puddles.

The captain found the cooperative chairman. They stood in a muddy farmyard and the chairman, twisting his fur cap in his hands, complained that he had not made deliveries because rats and worms had eaten the stocks of grain before they could be sent to the mill. The officer listened with his head on one side and then said:

- Worms? I'm not so sure about worms, but rats got in. I'm sure of that. But where did they get in? Through a hole in the wall? No. They got in through the front door. You left the door open, didn't you?

- Yes, well.... the lock is broken, you see. I've made a request, lots of requests but...

Hmm. A request for repairs? If you took a piece of wire you could fix the door yourself. Just a length of wire around the handles would do the trick. Why didn't you do that?

Everyone looked into the darkness of the barn.

- I said: Why didn't you do that?

The chairman shuffled his feet and looked around.

- Well...

There was no answer.

- You could have used a length of bailing wire. See, it's lying all over the place.

- Yes, I suppose...

- So.... How much grain do you think these rats of yours ate? It seems they ate rather a lot. I looked in your barn and I can't find any trace of grain at all.... They must have been very big rats. Very hungry rats. On two legs, I think...[19]

---

[19]Corruption was an integral part of Polish life at this time. In 1970 Party First Secretary Edward Gierek, having secured massive hard currency investment loans from western banks, said to the Poles: 'Enrich yourselves'. Most Poles did not have the opportunity, but for more than a decade the Party and its functionaries did. By May 1981, as Solidarność and the military began to get to grips with the full extent of corruption, 13 Government Ministers, 40 Deputy Ministers,

The officer turned away and began to walk towards the farmhouse.

- Yes, he said over his shoulder. I think we'll have a look at your account books. And then I think we'll take a look at your bank account...

Suddenly, running after the officer across the farmyard, the chairman commenced a long desperate wail on the difficulty of obtaining top quality wire.

- This stuff lying about is no good, it would not last ten minutes, but the good stuff, all the good stuff I had, the really good stuff all got stolen. You don't know what it's like around here. They steal everything. Everything...

The officer stopped and turned.

- Is that so?

valentine's day

St Valentine's Day. No cards. Sigh. Just back from a course in Stegna. Too tired to do anything but sit in the bath. My local shop has closed down. All the goods [hah!] have been removed and there is a big sign on the door saying that it is due for redecoration. There is no sign of

---

18 Regional Governors, 26 Deputy Regional Governors, 26 Regional Party First Secretaries, 72 Regional Party Secretaries, 7 Heads of government department, 8 Parliamentary Deputies and 14 Directors of major industrial enterprises, the Party First Secretary, the Prime Minister, and Trades Union Chief and his three assistants had all been sacked and faced legal proceedings. Two ministers committed suicide. Jaruzelski's anti-corruption drive, of which the idea of putting soldiers into the villages was a part, was too little and far too late to make any real or immediate difference to the economic life of the country.

any work though. This is a real blow to the neighbourhood. We relied on the store for yogurt, apples and bread - though mostly they only had bay leaves and vinegar for sale. Now the nearest shop, also specialising in bay leaves and vinegar, is about half a mile away.

There is an occupation strike of the building where I work. The strike is in sympathy with students in Łódź who want to form their own branch of Solidarność, but who were being prevented by the authorities. Clearly the Łódź strike is a test case for students across Poland.

When I arrive at work the gates to the building are chained shut and there is a guard of students. As well as all the usual banners and flags there is one that reads: 'Freedom for Political Prisoners'. I speak in English to the students at the door and tell them I am a journalist. Grudgingly they let me in and I am conducted through the packed entrance hall to an office. One of the stewards says he is sorry if anybody was rude to me at the gate, but they expect the security services to try and get in, to do damage and steal files and equipment, to compromise the students and make them look like a bunch of hooligans. He says they have been warned that the secret milicja in Łódź have already stolen typewriters and tape recorders. We talk for an hour, wandering through the crowd. He picks out people to tell me stories and verify facts. When I asked what the students wanted Student Solidarność to do for them their reply was ready:

- We want our MA degree to be a real degree, a useful professional qualification. We know, instead, that after four years of study we have something that is not recognised outside Poland. We spend too much time on Marxist philosophy and civil defence and physical education. We don't have the facilities to develop real professional expertise in our chosen fields. Also we want to remove the compulsory study of Russian. Nobody wants Russian classes.

Suddenly a cry went up and the Dean arrived saying he wanted to address the students in the hall. The hall is probably the worst place in the world to address tense and angry students. Poorly lit, but nevertheless beautiful to look at, with arches and angles, wide stair cases and corridors running off into the distance. The acoustic of the place is entirely unpredictable: voices boom and roar, are muffled and lost entirely. The Dean speaks to the students for about half an hour in slow measured tones. When he has finished there is some applause. One of the students stands up and says:

- We thank you for your courage in coming here, sir. As you can see we are not anti-socialist wreckers, and the people's property is being treated with great respect. However, what you have said does not alter our resolve. We want the best for Poland and for our children. You said everything will be attended to, but with respect we don't think this is likely. If things need altering it is we who must do it, not the authorities who created the mess in the first place.

The Dean's face hardly flickers. He says quietly:
- These things take time. You cannot rush them.

Somebody in the body of the hall shouts:
- We have run out of time. Now is the last chance we have to carry out reforms. We will be left behind completely while the rest of the world is in the twenty first century.

The Dean looks old and stooped and grey in the dim hallway light. His currency is exhausted. The students are right and he knows it.

Burning Worm

After he has gone, in the main entrance hall of the university, student strikers whisper in groups. Every so often a pale face rises from the huddle, looks around to see who is watching, then goes back to the discussion.

*

Later I bumped into Henryk, a local lawyer, and as we were on nodding terms from the university, we decided to sit together for lunch. I was amazed that he knew of a restaurant that still had anything to serve, so this was not an opportunity I would miss. He worked as an advisor to Solidarność and had cut his teeth working with KOR in the late 1970s.[20] After a few minutes we were joined by another colleague, a surgeon called Mirek, crumpled with fatigue. Mirek told us about a case he had dealt with during the night.

- A drunk. The milicja found him lying in a field. Somebody had tried to cut his balls off. Please forgive the indelicacy. But that's how it was. And they very nearly succeeded too. His scrotum was cut right the way round and his balls were hanging out. How they weren't cut off I'll never know. And it was a good clean cut too. Must have used a scalpel or a razor. Anyway I stitched him up. Probably he'll be OK. When he came round this morning I spoke to him. The last thing he could remember was going

[20] KOR: Komitet Obrony Robotnikow: Committee Defending Workers. Founded in September 1976 after protesting workers in Radom and at the Ursus tractor factory were victimised by the authorities. In spite of severe milicja harassment KOR gathered and published materials relating to human rights abuses. It also defended workers in court. KOR disbanded itself in 1981 saying its work had been completed with the birth of Solidarność. [See also pages 164-65.]

into the field with a prostitute. He was complaining because she had robbed him. He didn't seem bothered by the fact she had nearly castrated him, just complained about the money. I told him that if the prostitute did it, the fact that she chose some freezing field probably saved him from bleeding to death. His wife came in to visit later. She didn't seem in the least bit concerned either. The lives some people lead...

He got up to leave.

- Won't you stay and eat with us?

- Eat? No appetite. Too tired. I have three hours to sleep before I am due back. I must go home and get clean clothes, at least...

We all shook hands and Mirek left. A few days later I heard he had been sent home from work. Mirek, poised to start cutting with a scalpel in his hand, had begun to shake uncontrollably. The head surgeon accused him of drinking on duty.

The soldiers at the next table were eating *galonka* - whole boiled leg of pork - with mashed potato and sauerkraut and mustard, washed down with beer. One had loosened his tie, taken off his jacket and was loudly toasting his mate's sister. As we sat down a waiter placed two wobbling portions of chicken in jelly on the table in front of us. I asked:

- Can we have a menu please.

The waiter shrugged and walked away leaving the chicken.

- Well, said Henryk, adjusting his glasses in a way that only lawyers can. You've had a few months with us now. So how do you find our Solidarność?

- Solidarność? It's difficult to say what's going on, without even beginning to pass an opinion. Whatever it is they are doing I wish they'd hurry up and do it. It's taking them forever to do anything at all. I mean they're nice to have around, but things can't carry on like this forever, can they? They aren't really a trades union. Not in the western sense. And they aren't a political party either. But time is running out. They will have to become a political party, I think, in order to become a trades union. Will the Russians allow them to become a political Party though? Not if Solidarność moves slowly; the more slowly they move the less chance there is they will be able to offer any reassurance to the Soviet Union, and the more chance there is the Stalinists in the Polish Party will make the phone call asking for fraternal assistance from the USSR...

Henryk laughed and rearranged the cutlery nervously. He looked at me through his thick glasses.

- A typical western response. Solidarność must go at its own pace. We have a lot to learn. We hurry slowly. That's how it should be with democracy, no?

- Yes, but the army.... something is happening.

- The Polish army is absolutely trustworthy, believe me. They will protect us. They would never move against us. They would not dare. They are Poles. It would be a disaster for them even to try. But what am I saying. It is unthinkable. They have mothers and fathers, brothers and sisters, all in Solidarność. Look at them, here, do they look as if they are preparing a putsch?

I thought there is a peculiar equation at work here. Solidarność believes its own propaganda and the Party cannot read the writing on the wall. Henryk spoke again:

- My legal work at the moment is entirely for Solidarność. Fine work, believe me, but exhausting. I go home to change my clothes, I feel I haven't seen my wife for weeks. But it's the same for her too. We have to go back to first principles. Basically Poland had a fine constitution and legal system, but it is ignored, subverted by the Party to its own ends. All our liberties are subsumed by the notion of national interest - and that just means the survival of the ruling clique. We have to reestablish all the rights guaranteed by our constitution. We have to break the idea that the Party is above the law, that Poland is a vassal state of the USSR We have to behave as if we lived in a free country. And why not? Our law says we are free. So we stick to the law, and let the authorities show their power, if that is all they can use to coerce us. I'm dying with tiredness. I have more work in a month than I used to deal with in a year. The courts are jammed solid with appeals and claims. You see they try to dismiss activists from their jobs on all sorts of stupid trumped up charges, and we have to defend them all, of course. We can't let them get away with a thing. The only case we won't touch is where someone is dismissed for drinking at work. If that is proven, or the victim admits to it, we just say no. We're very strong on that. Booze is such a demoralising agent. The Church and Solidarność agree on this. You see, the Party undermines our morality, our morale, our discontent, our determination to change things by providing cheap alcohol. We have to be responsible for ourselves.

I nodded without much sympathy. Solidarność had curbed the sale of alcohol. I had not had a drink for over five months. On the wall behind Henryk a handwritten notice said that vodka was reserved only for officers in uniform.

The waiter ambled over to us.

- Hurry up. Other people got to eat. There's a queue.

- Is this it? Nothing else? said Henryk. How about the *galonka*?

But the waiter was not listening, indeed he was already out of earshot.

- Fucking worm, said Henryk, glaring at the waiter's back. Of course Poland is heading for a return to Europe, to European standards of behaviour, rather than Asiatic standards. We are, even at this late date, while the west heads for the twenty first century, heading for the twentieth century.... Well, perhaps that is too ambitious. But we are at least heading for the start of the twentieth century. He looked in the direction of the waiter. Of course, after so many years of Soviet influence, some of us may have further to travel than others, but still ....

Outside the sun was trying to shine. We looked balefully at the chicken in jelly wobbling on the table and picked up our knives and forks.

Later Henryk and I wandered past the steps of the university administration building. A small bookstall had sprung up. Students were selling pamphlets. Like everyone else we wanted to see what was on offer: 'Piłsudski and his Generals', 'Sikorski: Assassinated by the British?', 'Why Was Warsaw destroyed', 'Katyn', 'Poland's lost years'. There was an atmosphere of political pornography about all this. Something salacious. The dearth of honesty, the pathological secrecy of the Party, the corruption of folk lore all caused a terrible intellectual thirst. Henryk pointed out quietly that purchase was furtive: a wad of notes thrust into a hand, pamphlets pushed into a raincoat pocket, then the buyer was off.

- You see, said Henryk. In their mind it is still not quite legal.

Somewhere along the street, in a doorway, the buyer would take out the purchase, skim through the pages, then with a lick of the lips and a glance around to see if anyone was watching, head off home at top speed. Henryk bought a small pamphlet on Piłsudski and went back to work.

*

I went with a couple of new friends to a nightclub. None of us had much money. Harry and I worked for Polish currency, and our Swedish companion, Olaf, was the worst paid worker in the Gdańsk shipyard. Olaf was also the youngest and smallest Swede working in Poland. However, regardless of our problems, the very fact that we were so obviously foreign in our appearance was enough to get us into the nightclub for free.

The club was dimly lit, and each booth was decked out with hideous plastic fruit, probably supplied by some returning sailor at a ridiculous price. The dance floor, unlike the rest of the place, was washed by ultraviolet light - the slightest speck of dandruff on the dancers showed up brilliant white.

We found a booth lit by a dim red lamp and ordered drinks - soft, of course. Olaf started to eye up an enormous Polish girl with a bobbing bottled blond ponytail. She was at least three times Olaf's weight, and even though Harry and I were both around six foot, I believe she was taller than that. She was also, clearly, a prostitute. We tried to tell Olaf, but he did not want to hear it and eventually he caught her eye and called her over. Her conversation - a mixture of Polish, German, French, English and Swedish - was packed with innuendo from the start, and what she could not say in words, she indicated with her hands or her eyebrows. It took her only a few moments to realise that Olaf was the mark, and it was only a few moments more before she had slid close up beside him and begun to unzip his fly beneath the table.

Olaf did not speak much Polish. I said to the girl in Polish:
- He has no hard currency. He can only pay in zloty.
- Ask her how much, said Olaf.
- What, no dollars, no kroner?
- No. No hard currency at all.
- How much did she say?
- None at all?
- You are holding the hardest thing the man owns right now.

Turning in her seat she let go of Olaf's penis and let rip with a string of obscenities in all the languages known to her. She finished off by giving Olaf a slap across the mouth so hard that it drew blood in a vivid spurt. She rose from our table and stalked away, but in the middle of the dance floor, a distance of some eight or nine feet from our table, she turned and spat. A little gobbet of hot phlegm landed precisely in Olaf's drink.

Nobody in the club took much notice of the incident. The blond left the club at a run. A German sailor in his early twenties monopolised the dance floor with a vigorous, simple and repetitive dance-solo. His hand-clapping and foot crashing made the music irrelevant.

We cleaned Olaf up, and then calmed him down. After a few minutes we began to laugh at the incident. It was only when a slightly recovered Olaf reached for his money to order another round of drinks that he realised she had lifted his wallet. A moment later he realised she had taken his wristwatch as well. A real smooth operator.

warning strike

24 March 1981. Listening to the radio. Some kind of a row within the Party. Stefan Bratkowski and Mieczysław Rakowski have offered to resign from the Central Committee. But why? The western stations refer to Rakowski, who is the senior editor of the Party journal *Polityka*, as a liberal and a moderate. So are we to suppose that the Party is now leaning towards the hard-liners in some way? And anyway what does it mean to say that a member of the Central Committee is a moderate. He may be more open to negotiation and prepared to voice criticisms, but he wouldn't be on the Central Committee if he were a serious liberal of any standing or conviction. He will always do as the Party bids him. Compared to some of the harder hard-liners he may be willing to take a more conciliatory line, but he's not about to offer power sharing to Solidarność, that's for sure. So what does it mean to say he's a liberal or a moderate. That he can hold a conversation? That he will listen to the other side before doing what he wants to do regardless? But why are we being told this at all? And is it true? They give us the facts but they don't give a clue as to what the facts might mean. It is a power struggle, witnessed through a fog, with the sounds of battle dulled and muffled by the media. And when it is over we will not be any wiser.

Burning Worm

*

Last night I was invited to watch a video. It was a copy of the milicja record of events in Bydgoszcz. It seems that the secret milicja have badly beaten about twenty members of Solidarność during a meeting with the local council. The milicja - the regular uniformed milicja, who were also in attendance at the meeting - video taped much of the incident.

The tape was unedited and the sound quality was very poor, but as far as I can make out what happened was as follows.

Rural Solidarność had requested that several of its members be allowed to attend a local government council meeting. There was already a sit-in at Party headquarters pushing for full recognition of Rural Solidarność, but a group of the membership and their supporters thought they might help matters if they were allowed to lobby and debate with Party members at the council meeting. Those in attendance included Jan Rulewski, hotheaded member of KPN[21] and leader of Rural Solidarność, and Deputy Prime Minister Stanisław Mach. Everything seemed to have gone well when the Chairman suddenly closed the

---

[21]KPN: Konfederacja Polska Niepodległa: Confederation for an Independent Poland. A right wing, fundamentalist, nationalist, anti-Semitic organisation. Campaigning slogans included: 'Poland for the Poles' and 'Poland for Real Poles'. Between 1979 and 1981 KPN provided the bulk of Poland's political prisoners. The problem of whether or not Solidarność should campaign for the release of KPN leader Leszek Moczulski was much discussed. Eventually Solidarność decided that no matter how dangerous or wrong-headed they thought KPN might be, Poland should have no political prisoners. [See also page 150.]

meeting just as Solidarność members were about to speak. The decision took everybody by surprise and Solidarność and council members expressed a desire to stay on and talk. After a few minutes however, it seems Mach left the meeting and called the milicja, who were waiting nearby. The milicja arrived. This is where the video record begins. And after a polite exchange of opinions gave everybody fifteen minutes to clear the building.

It is not certain why the milicja were called. Nor is it clear why the milicja should have insisted on clearing the building. For me the important point was: why did the milicja take a video camera with them? Did the presence of a video camera indicate that they had planned this intervention? More likely that they were reluctant to do the job, expected complications and wanted to cover themselves.

What followed the expiry of the deadline was very confused. The milicja returned, but the councilors and the Solidarność members formed a circle and refused to leave. There was a lot of pushing and shoving, but no violence, and eventually everyone was bundled out of a side door. We did not see the next bit, but once outside the door, it seems, plain clothes members of the Department of Security had forced the Solidarność members to run 'the path of health', that is between two rows of truncheons.

The injured men were dragged back inside the building. We were shown pictures of Rulewski and about twenty others lying on the floor, waiting for ambulances to arrive. They had clearly been beaten. The uniformed milicja were at pains to point out that they were not responsible for the beatings. But Solidarność made the point that the beatings were illegal and the uniformed milicja, who are in fact a

Citizen's militia, should have intervened to offer protection.

The video is not a very enlightening document. It does not show the beatings, nor who was responsible. What it did show very effectively was the pain and shock of those who had been assaulted and the powerlessness of the uniformed milicja.

Today there are posters everywhere displaying the bruised, bloody, toothless face of Jan Rulewski. There is talk of a general strike. Solidarność is calling for an inquiry into the events in Bydgoszcz, but as usual the government are dragging their feet. Solidarność want this strike very badly, not just in retaliation for the beatings, but for all the instances of bad faith over the last few months. However, their feeling is that a general strike could get out of hand. Possibly the secret milicja could stage a few incidents to make it look as if it were out of control. In this case a general strike would be followed by serious violence. Solidarność know that people are losing faith in them, that beyond their existence, they have nothing practical to show for themselves. Solidarność is dealing with a melting support base.

How Solidarność deals with the matter of the beatings is the real crisis point. Not the registration crisis or the invasion scare. This is the pivot. March 27 1981 was a half-day warning strike. The government's failure to find and arrest the culprits means that they have not taken heed of the warning. A General Strike was to follow.

We were supposed to start a new course at Janowice that day, which meant we should have been loading the bus, taking the students out to the village at the exact moment the strike was due to start. I asked around among the teachers. I was surprised to learn that none of the teachers were planning to heed the strike call. They offered a variety of reasons: they were not engaged in productive labour, they were invisible, traveling is not working, that they were not members of Solidarność.... I replied that I was not a member of Solidarność - my membership application, I had been informed, was held up, pending, because I was a foreigner. Still I tried to say how important I thought this strike was. That even though I do not like KPN, I have to support Rulewski against this violence. That I find it very hard to cross a picket line, or to persuade others to do so. That I would not disobey a call to a general strike on such a clear cut matter of principle. The teachers laugh at me. You want to teach us about socialism? What a joke! Later someone said:

- Don't worry, we've found a driver for the bus. He admires the strong leadership of Mrs Thatcher and he won't be on strike. And if you get onto the bus a few minutes early, before the strike starts, you can put your feet up and have your own little sit-down strike all the way to Janowice. We should arrive there just as the strike finishes, so you won't compromise any of your beloved principles. Right?

- Well that's Kraków for you, I replied. Conservative in every way. Perhaps we could arrange a swap. Mrs Thatcher could be your Prime Minister and Lech Wałęsa could run the British trades unions. What do you think?

The strike was due to start at midday, but I wasn't sure that it would actually go ahead; perhaps Solidarność would achieve a breakthrough. I took my bag and went to the meeting place. I helped load the bus, determined that if the hooters announcing the start of the strike sounded I would cease immediately. As we loaded the last suitcase onto the luggage rack the factory hooters and car horns began to sound. Trams slowed to a stop, buses pulled over to the side of the road, the drivers assembled in clumps, they stood around with their hands in their pockets, smiling, or they lit up their cigarettes. The Polish flag was everywhere. A hush descended on the city. I said:

- OK. Go if you're going. I'll take the train when the strike is over.

I walked off through the slush to the office to see what was happening there. As I entered the office Janina, a staunch Party member, said:

- What are you doing at work? Don't you know there's a strike on? Go home.

The warning strike passed off without incident and I joined my course later that night. We began to focus on the coming general strike, but two days later it emerged that Wałęsa had done some kind of a private deal with the government. Without consulting Solidarność he canceled the planned general strike. I kept asking the teachers and students, what is happening, what does it mean, but they just shrugged. Too tired to care. The general strike built everybody up, then left everyone flat.

*

31 March 1981. Poland was first item again on the BBC World Service. A row within Solidarność, but no details as yet. Resignations: Modzelewski, who has said that Wałęsa is acting like a king, Gwiazda, Lis, Bujak, Walentinowicz, all of them founder members of Solidarność. I can hardly believe this is possible. Maybe it is related to the Bydgoszcz affair and the fact that Wałęsa called off the general strike without proper authority. But how? There are no details, so we really cannot be sure. I

can't work it out, and I can't find anyone else who can make sense of it either. I keep asking, why the resignations, what do they mean, but all I get is a shrug. Nobody knows, and worse, now nobody really gives a damn either. The decision to cancel the general strike without any satisfactory solution to the events in Bydgoszcz has left everybody absolutely flat and a little suspicious of Wałęsa. At the bus stop today somebody referred to him as King Wałęsa and no-one leapt to his defence. People are asking, what kind of a deal has he made? Why did he make it in private, why no consultation, what kind of democracy is that? This feels like a turning point of some sort. Again, something has shifted, changed, but what? Whatever it is, it's not visible yet. In Poland it seems, even with Solidarność, you can never know a thing for sure.

I hear that the office of Censors has petitioned the government, asking to be dissolved. Can that be true? Censorship, over a long period, has made all information scarce and untrustworthy. It has also put a premium on gossip and rumour. But such a situation robs everyone of a context for decision making. If you can't make sense of anything, how can you decide what to do? For example, I once met the manager of a small nail factory in Silesia. He complained to me that he was required to submit production and consumption statistics to Warsaw every month, but once he had done so he had no access to that information. I could scarcely believe it, but he was adamant: he had no access to his own factory's production figures. How is it possible to run a business like that, I asked. He shrugged. 'You can't run it as a business. I don't know what it is, but it is not a business.

Now, along the same lines, we have heard *plotki*[22] that the team of Polish negotiators went to speak with the West German Credit Banks, the World Bank and the IMF, to request the rescheduling of Poland's loan repayments due in 1981 and to request an extension for further loans. When the western banks asked the negotiators how the additional loans would be spent, so that they could ensure the projects would produce a big enough return to repay the loan, the negotiators said they had no information on this point. The western bankers asked the Polish team just what had happened to the $29,000,000,000 they had already sunk into the Polish economy, and why they should be expected to spend even more money in order to recoup the original loans, the Polish team had to admit once again that they had no information on these points. When pressed, they had to admit that they had no access to such information. It is rumoured - again! - that before they left Warsaw the Polish negotiators had approached the Ministry of Information for details of the case they were to argue in the west, only to be told that information of this kind was classified a National Secret and could certainly not be passed on to them lest it should fall into the hands of some foreign power and be used to harm Poland. This information was not publicly available anywhere in Poland. The negotiators did not know the size of the initial Polish debt until they read about it in the western press, and were told about it by the western bankers. I cannot say how true the story is, but it has a ring of truth about it - and not only that element of stupidity engendered by censorship, but also that element of approaching someone who is clearly willing to help, while suspecting that their help will only lead you further

---

[22] *Plotki* - gossip.

along the road to your doom. In Poland you can never know a thing for certain. It is like living in a hall of mirrors.

invasion

On the BBC World Service, US Secretary of State General Haig has again warned of a possible Soviet invasion of Poland, saying spy satellites have spotted Soviet troop movements along the Ukrainian/Polish border...

Hearing noises
In the night
Shouting
Engines revving
I feared war had broken out
Stumbling out of bed
I grabbed my passport
And made for the window
At the very least I thought
A tank
Cocktails Molotov at thirty paces
A new alphabet to learn
But
No star marked tank[23]
No decorated Ivan
[First or Second class]
Only those bastard dustmen
Working the early shift

---

[23]This is puzzling. Hinks almost certainly knew it was a western misconception. Warsaw Pact tanks were not decorated with a red star but used a broad white stripe, running from front to back, for purposes of aerial recognition.

Burning Worm

*

Deputy Premier Jagielski, during the shipyard negotiations, and General Jaruzelski just after he became Prime Minister both said they wanted to talk with the opposition 'Pole to Pole'. As if they believed that the life of the nation took precedence over all ideological considerations of left and right, over corruption, violence and repression. And yet the situation is desperate. And the life of the Polish state is threatened. By hard liners in the Kremlin, by East Germany, by anarchy and chaos, by hunger and disease.

*

Now let us talk
Pole to Pole
Or
Else[24]

*

Standing at the bus stop. Seven o clock in the morning. A clear blue spring sky, birds singing. A hint of green on the trees. Cold dust on the roads. A helicopter scuds noisily over the rooftops to land in the barrack-square. A squad of about thirty paratroopers in combat fatigues and maroon berets approach along the road. They march four

---

[24]The phrase 'Pole to Pole' was used repeatedly, and in bad faith, by the government side in the shipyard negotiations of August 1980. Later it was used by the representatives of General Jaruzelski's civilian government just before the declaration of Martial Law.

abreast with an officer at the head of the column and a rear marker with a flag. They swing past us with a long even tread, guns at the trail, their packs dragging on their backs. They look exhausted. All traffic stops for them at the intersection, they tramp across, swing left and then right into the front entrance of the barracks. Everyone watches them pass. The man next to me says:

- There they go, the boys.

*

At the end of March 1981 the Invasion Scare was still going strong. Night after night on just about every western radio station US General Haig screeched his warnings. I didn't need him to tell me that the situation was likely to go sky high at any moment. The Polish army was making preparations of its own. At the time it appeared that they were preparing to defend Poland against external aggression. It was only later that we came to understand that they were also making ready for an entirely different sort of operation. At the end of March I reasoned that if the Russians were foolish enough to invade they would do so either while the ground was still hard, or after the Polish spring thaw, when the ground had firmed up enough to permit the easy passage of tanks across open countryside.

Why should I have feared a Russian invasion so much? Well anyone in their right mind fears to be at the centre of a military action.

But I had to do something that winter. It was urgent. I had to find a focus for my energy, a point to my day. I needed something to do apart from sitting and waiting for the BBC World Service news broadcasts. I had a television that did not work. I had no social circle because I was always out of town on courses. Likewise for most of the time I had no girl friend. I had read all the books I had brought with me, and had ransacked the British Council Library for more. For months I kept a diary. Meticulously. Night after night I would sit down at my table by the light of the rolling TV screen, and scribble down as much as I could make sense of from the day's events. I was never very happy with my journal. I realised that I had captured some of the mood of Poland, but I was also aware that I had not captured everything I sought to relate. The landscape I presented was also that of my mental state. I saw Solidarność and Poland through my own frustrations, depression, loneliness and hunger. Perhaps it was a state of mind, after all. But there is another way to look at it. Perhaps what I wrote was accurate enough, and the country merely reflected, by some odd coincidence, the feelings I had. Perhaps this was the state of Poland. Is it possible for a country to read a state of mind? Must it always be an individual's interpretation of a country? Is it ever possible to avoid the subjective? and still convey the immediacy, the sense of how it was to live in that place, in that time, in that way? What a state to be in.

I had also written dozens of letters, but never once managed to get close to describing how Poland - or I - felt, never managed to make the chaos mean anything to anyone else: the replies were always bland, blank, uncomprehending. I had given up writing letters. Instead I thought a great deal about past relationships, about my family, about why I had come to be here, in Poland, at this particular moment. But this was not enough to occupy my mind.

In class one day I used a tape recording of the previous night's news broadcast from the BBC as a listening comprehension. The effect on the class was electrifying. I never had a more devoted and attentive group of students. The next day another group requested the same lesson. And a few days later one of the students very quietly suggested that transcripts of this material would be very useful, not as teaching materials, but as information for Solidarność. He suggested I should make tapes, or better still transcripts, available to Solidarność:

- It is very important to us to know how the rest of the world sees us and how they report what is happening here.

And that is how it started. From then on I spent most of my evenings at home waiting for the BBC news at 10.00, or searching the airwaves for other news broadcasts. Each night I made a tape recording of the news, then typed up a transcript. I listened in to almost every European English language news service: Radio Prague, Radio Free Europe, Voice of America, Radio Luxembourg. For a little light relief I also listened to the Albanian Radio Tirana - a station which, if it had not been so boring, would have been the joke station of all time. It was rare that I managed to get to the end of any broadcast from Radio Tirana: the announcer's voice was so un-inflected that I usually switched off out of sheer boredom. Once I picked up an Israeli broadcast, and once a broadcast from South Africa.

I took the transcripts with me on the bus and dropped them off for Henjak to collect at the Mała Polska headquarters of Solidarność, just opposite the Kijów cinema, on my way to work. There was no fuss, no bother. I don't know what became of the transcripts or what use they made of them. They were just my contribution to the *Odnowa* or renewal. If I didn't show up nobody asked why.

It occurred to me later that if I had been arrested for this activity Solidarność would not have known about it, probably would not have checked. When I stopped making transcripts nobody questioned my decision, nobody tried to persuade me to continue. I'm not even sure they noticed I had stopped. But by then things were getting very difficult indeed.

The question of how Solidarność was presented in the foreign press and media was merely academic. Food shortages, the row over the beatings in Bydgoszcz, rows about the Solidarność leadership, plans for the first Solidarność Congress, repeated confrontation with the authorities, the launch of the union's own newspaper were all far more pressing. Indeed, as the situation unraveled the western media became increasingly unable to offer any sensible comment, and it became more and more difficult to match up what I heard on foreign radio with what I saw around me.

It was not exactly a secret, but I told no-one what I was doing. Even so I worried that if there was an invasion my transcripts could be used against me. I had never signed them, it is true, but they could have been traced to me without too much difficulty. Perhaps they could say that I was using the broadcasts for propaganda purposes. Once you start you can make a case fit to frighten the pants off yourself. The Poles are pragmatists: they might lock me up to sell me for hard currency in a couple of years. But the Russians, if they didn't shoot me for spying, would probably pack me off to the GULAG - they really wouldn't waste time looking for evidence - and I did not imagine for one moment that I would survive that experience.

I knew that it would probably take some time for the Russian or Polish authorities to trace the author of the transcripts, and that they would have far more pressing problems on their minds at first, but it seemed better to be safe than sorry. I had a box of matches I had been hoarding specially for this purpose. So, in March 1981 I determined to destroy anything that might incriminate me. Notes, papers, letters, photographs, documents relating to Solidarność, dissident literature, and even a few Party documents that had come my way.

I collected all papers and documents from my flat and put them in a bag. Then I went for a long walk in the woods. There was a spot I had noticed where someone had made a bonfire some weeks before. The ash from my notebooks would not be noticed here.

I scouted round, made sure no-one was nearby, then set the pages alight, one by one. The flames took them all - diaries, addresses, notebooks, jottings, newspaper clippings. It was a long job. Last to go were the copies of the radio transcripts I had made for Solidarność. I had been glad to have a focus, a role, something to do. Probably the transcripts were the only thing I could do as a foreigner. I had taken great care with the work, typed neatly, kept carbons. I was reluctant to destroy them. They were my contribution, however mysterious, to Poland's peaceful revolution. But no, they had to go. I fed the flames. Ash floated up, and a greasy flame licked the trees. I warmed my hands by the blaze, then when the flame died down, took a stick and stirred the ash so no sizable fragment survived. Then I scattered the ash around with my foot, kicking clouds of embers in all directions.[25]

On my way home I took a long and circuitous route through the woods. As I emerged from the trees a military convoy thrashed through the village, throwing sheets of mud in all directions and scattering the children. Only when I was sure they were not stopping did I venture out of the woods.

*

Peace Monument
Bristling armoured monster
Anchored to a foot of stone
Hedged with bristling bayonets
The heroes
Jaws firm and square
Muscle slabs under workers shirts
His gaze on distant enemies
Her gaze on him
His best girl by his side

---

[25] Hinks may inadvertently have been of use to both sides. Although he does not name the person who recruited him into the radio monitoring scheme, it seems likely it was Dr Henryk Henjak, a lecturer in the Department for the Protection of Intellectual Property Rights and a leading member of the University branch of Solidarność. Later Henjak was suspected of being an informer. It is possible the reason Hinks remained undisturbed by the Security Service was that Henjak was showing them Hinks' transcripts. The Security Service were as desperate as Solidarność for information, and Hinks was one of the few sources available. Henjak had no difficulty obtaining a passport and left Poland in 1984 to take up a post at a Midwestern university in the USA.

Burning Worm

Roundabout the earth
Slippery with wounds
Even a peace monument
Is a kind of
Folly

*

All night military transport planes had droned into the airport. In the early hours of the morning huge trains laden with tanks and amphibious vehicles rumbled past my window. The barracks over the road was full to bursting and the lights burned late. I had lain in bed wondering, twitching. I was jumpy as hell, but later I went into the centre of Kraków and after an hour or so of mooching about I finally managed to buy some fresh eggs. Whatever happened today, I had eggs. So maybe it wouldn't be too bad after all. At least I could eat.

I put the eggs in my string bag and began to walk across the central square towards the Sukiennice.[26] Movement away to my left, at the angle of the square, caught my eye. From a side road a squat drab green tank maneuvered into the square like a clumsy toad. Its tracks struck sparks from the cobbles, and as it bounced to a halt the gun began to traverse. The hypnotic fascination of the beast was broken when the gun stopped moving and it was pointed right at me.

I thought, shit. This is it. This is *it*. Then I began to run. All around me people were running, screaming, ducking into doorways, diving for cover. Ahead of me an old woman fell spraying her purchases all over the pavement. A friend helped her up and they ran on. We

---

[26] *Sukiennice* - Cloth Market Hall.

headed for the arcaded front of the Cloth hall. Dodging in between the arches I tried to get my breath.

After a moment I peeped out. The tank was still there, but it had not fired. Across the square were scattered hats and gloves, shoes, a chicken, potatoes, heads of garlic. A man was crawling towards the arcade on his hands and knees while his friends called to him. There was blood on his face. All along the inside of the arcade people were breathing hard, slumped against the brickwork, or peering round the columns. Not far away a man was lying at full length while someone listened to his chest. Behind, a woman was hammering at the locked door of a shop, screaming:

- Call an ambulance! It's a heart attack! A heart attack! Please call an ambulance! Please!

The man on the floor was grey. Someone said:

- Why don't the bastards shoot? It's what they came here to do.

I took another look. The tank was still there. Then someone further along the arcade shouted:

- Hey, it's got a white eagle on the turret. It must be one of ours.[27]

At almost the same moment the hatch on the tank flew open and a soldier climbed out, waving his hand and grinning. A milicja car nosed into the square, its lights flashing. A loudspeaker on the milicja car boomed a message:

- Citizens! Do not be afraid. Do not panic. Go about your business. Go about your duties. This is an old tank from the war. There is no cause for alarm. It is being used in a

---

[27]The Polish white eagle - royal crown removed - was used to mark the tanks of Polish communist forces under General Berling in World War II.

film about the life of the Pope. Do not panic. Go about your business.

Behind me somebody breathed:

- Sons of bitches.

The woman was still banging on the door:

- Call an ambulance somebody please.

The man on the floor looked dead.

It was a long time before anybody moved out from the arcade. Eventually I found the courage, after others had already done so, and went over to find my shopping bag. The eggs were smashed. Children were already swarming over the tank. In the distance I could hear an ambulance siren.

april fool

Waiting for me when I got home, wedged in the door jamb, was a telegram. From Marie-Therese of all people. I unlocked the front door, staggered into the hallway, dumped my bags and opened the telegram. It read:

- Arriving Poland 13.00. April 1st. Meet me. Marie-Therese.

I looked at the calendar. Today was April 1st. But where was she arriving, and how? Where was I to meet her? The railway station, bus station, the airport? In Poznań? Warsaw? I had no idea.

I made tea and stood on my balcony, breathing the sharp spring air. Column after column of troops marched in and out of the barracks opposite. A helicopter thrashed over the treetops and clattered down onto the parade ground. Paratroopers lounged at the open windows reading comics and calling to passing girls.

Burning Worm

We had parted company the previous summer - though I don't think either of us realised we had actually parted. When I heard about my new job in Kraków we borrowed a friend's apartment in Paris for the weekend bought a bottle of champagne and celebrated. Later we posed for photographs. I remember August heat in the apartment, the smooth tan curve of her body against the dark tear drop pattern of the covers. We developed the prints in the bathroom, were surprised and delighted with the pictures. I hung enlargements around the place to dry. More by accident than design I had produced something pleasing. The pictures captured, even enhanced, a precise and alluring image. Marie-Therese was fascinated by them. She stood naked on the cool linoleum in the bathroom doorway, one foot on top of the other, her tongue between her teeth, her eyes narrowed till they looked like currants in pastry. There was an unusual intensity about the way she looked at these pictures. The photographs informed her of something. There was no going back on it. I had learned to live with her complicated attitudes to men; but the photographs - my own pictures - defeated me. The pictures showed us as a man and a woman, heavenly bodies, things remote in time and space, in temporary mutual orbit, and then moving apart at considerable velocity, subject to different laws. These images overwhelmed us with our difference, our otherness. She took the pictures as a liberation, an opening to all the other loves and lovers she might have. Looking back - and hindsight is a precise science - we were finished. It was there in the pictures.

She insisted she would join me in Poland. I spent a great deal of time running around trying to fix her a teaching job. After several meetings and the prolonged perusal of her CV by the Polish Ministry of Education, she was finally offered a place teaching French at Kraków University. However, on the same December day I heard about her appointment I also received a long, abject letter from her saying that it was unrealistic to think she could move to Poland, she now had a good job in Paris, that I should realise there was a political struggle going on in France too. The double talk could be summarised: I have a new boyfriend. I heard nothing more from her for months. Now there was a telegram.

I ran a bath, and lying in the soapy water decided the telegram was an April Fool joke. In the early hours of the next morning my door bell rang and there on the mat stood Marie-Therese. I kissed her politely on the cheek. She said:

- Aha! So, I find you. Me. All by my ownself.

I tipped the taxi driver for carrying her luggage up four floors. It was only when I came to lift her bags I realised my tip was quite inadequate. It was as if her bags had been nailed to the floor.

- I send a telegram.

- Yes.

- So, why you don't meet me?

- You didn't say where. And you didn't say please.... Why didn't you write?

- Ah non I couldn't explain. This was best for me.

- Aha...

The visit, it was clear, had nothing to do with reconciliation.

- So?

She shrugged.

- I don't want you to have wrong idea of me here.

- I have no idea at all,' I said.

- My union. They ask me to come. It was their idea. They know I have contact in Poland, that I know someone here. They sended for me. I told them 'I am finish with him', but they say: If he is good comrade you explain him, he will understand. So they pay my train. They say me: 'Is free holiday.

- So we meet again courtesy of The Party, hmm?. How nice. Are you a member now?

She looked sheepish.

- But your new boyfriend is…

She shifted uneasily in her chair.

- You are angry. Will you hit me?

- You are thinking of someone else.

- Yes. I'm sorry to say that thing to you. You don't never hit me.

I made up a mattress on the living room floor.

- Is that how you want? Separate sleepings? It is not necessary.

- You want to sleep with me? Why? For the sake of the Party, maybe.

- Can you let me have soap and toothpaste?

- You can use whatever you find in the bathroom cupboard.

After a moment she stood in front of me, flicking her toothbrush with annoyance.

- Your cupboard. She is empty.

- I know. You see, there is no soap, no toothpaste in Poland. Don't you read the newspapers? Or maybe you only read Party newspapers. If you had written to me I could have told you, there is nothing here. Nothing. I would have said, bring everything you need.

She looked at me long and hard.

- Nothing? Hah! I don't believe.

Burning Worm

Next morning she unpacked her bags. I watched as she hauled out dozens of large format French language glossy publications. I flipped though them: *The Constitution of Solidarność. The Policies and Strategies of Solidarność, The History of Solidarność.* They were very heavy, superbly printed, lavishly illustrated, on very expensive paper. They must have cost a fortune. Marie-Therese smiled proudly.

- I smuggle them into Poland. Me, by my ownself.

- I can hardly believe you actually brought this stuff all the way from Paris.

- Oui. I was nerve in case they founded it...

- And what do you think they would do if they found it?

- Arrest me. Expel me. Oh la dissidence, oui? These book is forbid. Very dangerous stuffs...

- Dangerous? Oh it's dangerous alright. It nearly gave me a hernia. Somebody could die laughing, I suppose.

I dropped the books in a heap.

- Don't you know Solidarność is legal now? All this stuff is legal, it's allowed. And anyway, do you really think a Polish factory worker wants to read his union's constitution - in French? As soon as they spot that this is from the French Communist Party they'll lose interest; if they didn't use it to light the fire, they'd use it to wipe their arse.... There's no toilet paper here either, by the way. What a bloody stupid waste of an opportunity. You could have brought something useful. Medicine. Food. Tampons. Anaesthetics. Hypodermic needles. Surgical gloves. This stuff.... it's just.... shit.

Marie-Therese looked shocked.

- Did you bring anything of any bloody use at all? Food? Tea? Coffee? Alcohol?

- The Party say me the capitalist newspaper is lying about food shortage. The capitalists, they want to isolate this first genuine workers' revolution. I think you don't appreciate our manifestation of solidarity with Polish worker.
- Too bloody right I don't. And 35 million Poles will be equally unimpressed. Unless these magazines are edible...

We sat looking at the pile of magazines.

- What are you supposed to do with these things?
- I must to distributed them to Lesh Waleeza.
- Lesh Waleeza...? Oh, Lech Wałęsa. And how are you going to do that? He doesn't speak French and you don't speak Polish.
- What is matter with you? I never seed you like these before. I read about Easter 1916.... I thought, you are Irish, you will support, understand...
- Romantic guff!. Revolution is romantic from a distance.... but close to it's.... it's.... Damn it! Don't you know the Russians could invade at any moment? Shit! I'm tired, I'm frightened and I'm very, very hungry...
- They don't have Tampons? But my period is start tomorrow...

We sat in silence.

Poland was a blank place on the map for her. She had done no homework, had no idea how far Kraków was from Gdańsk. Everyday she asked me to take her to 'Lesh Waleeza', as if we could just drop in, like old friends. She was convinced that Poland was 'a little country'. I found a map to show her: the distance from Kraków to Gdańsk was the same as Marseilles to Le Havre. More than twelve hours by train. If there was a train. If we could get a ticket. If the train ran. If it ran on time. If the train completed the journey. Just the previous week I had heard of a train that was twenty four hours late.

I took her to the university and introduced her to the French language teachers. Marie-Therese hauled the magazines from her bag - 'Hey, Voila!' - slapping them down on a glass topped desk. Did she think the teachers would hug her and kiss her? They flipped through the magazines quickly, admiring the colour photographs, and then left them on the table. Marie-Therese could not understand. She could not get it into her head that her beautiful books were no big deal, that there was no risk in bringing them to Poland or in touting them about the place. She threatened to take them out onto the street to sell them on the Black Market. But I think she had begun to appreciate that the Black Market was busy with other things: the books remained in a sloppy heap on my sitting room floor, a sackful of political pornography.

One day Marie-Therese burst into tears, wailing:

- It is so depressive here in Poland. How you can stand it?

I knew exactly what she meant. But I had other thoughts too. Should I tell her about about Wawel Castle in the snow, the mountains above the mists, the gently rolling countryside, the smell of pine forests in summer, about willows standing in winter fogs, about wine and long conversations through the night, about poetry, about reading between the lines, about people forced to become ingenious beyond reason, about resistance in daily life, about people who make what they have work for them and who ask for no more than they need, should I contrast this with life in the West, point out that what she sees as lack of colour is actually the absence of advertising slogans and hoardings? Hypocrite, I told myself. Keep quiet, you worm. You are just like her. No better. Just better prepared, perhaps.

She still insisted I take her to Gdańsk to meet Lesh Waleeza. I was tired of saying no. We went to look at the railway timetable. She saw for herself nearly a third of the trains were not running, but she insisted we get tickets. We went to the booking hall and she gasped in horror at the queues: over a hundred people at each ticket window. We pushed and shoved our way into the right queue, waited over two hours to hear that there were no seats on any train to Gdańsk for at least a fortnight. The booking clerk said wearily:

- Everybody wants to go there. Since this Solidarność business started. Delegates, representatives, seeking advice, guidance. Why don't you take a plane?

So we went to the airline office and commenced to queue again. Eventually the woman behind the window listened patiently to my attempt at Polish and then said in beautiful, clear, precise English:

- I'm so sorry sir. There are no seats available on any plane to Gdańsk for nearly one month. If you really want to go you should buy a train ticket and stand in the corridor.

- OK then,' said Marie-Therese. 'That's what we do.

- No, I said. That's what *you* do. I'm not standing on a train for twelve hours just to deliver a pile of junk to Lesh Waleeza.

Marie-Therese, as best she could in the crush, turned on her heel and forced her way out of the office.

Next day when I returned from work I had a newspaper, a loaf and a jar of conserved fruit which one of the teachers had given me. It was four in the afternoon and I had had nothing to eat that day. Marie-Therese was sitting in the kitchen with a spoon in her hand.

- Your honey, she said. I ate it. I didn't like it. Not one teeny-tiny little bit, but anyway I ate it. All. I don't know why I do that

- But... I gasped. That was the last of the honey.

- Oh dear. I was so hungry. There was nothing for my breakfast. Never mind. Poor boy. Don't look so sad. You can get some more.

- There is no more fucking honey!

- Well, she giggled. So you get some jam...

I exploded.

- You giddy bitch! There is no fucking jam! I screamed. Don't you understand? There is no fucking anything in this country!

- So I can't help you, she said. Because I have eated all your honeys.

My stomach growled. She gave the spoon one last long lick.

Let me say a word about that honey. It was the only sweet thing I had been able to find. I had ration cards for sugar, but I never found any sugar to buy, and chocolate was available only for children. At the height of winter I had taken a train to a country town, I had taken a bus from the town to a nearby village. I had trudged through the snow from door to door, from farm to farm, asking to buy honey.

At last I found a farmer who kept bees. He said I was lucky, the city people had just about cleaned him out. He still had a little. But this was absolutely the last though. As he spoke mice scampered along the floor. One appeared on his kitchen table. He brushed it away affectionately with the back of his hand. He spooned the thick creamy honey into an old pickle jar, took a newspaper from the corner of the room, shook off the mouse turds, and wrapped the jar carefully.

I counted a huge sum of money into his callused hand. He explained that in the current economic situation Polish money was really of no use to him. I apologised for not having dollars, quickly bundled the honey into my string bag and carried it home, first through the village, then on the bus, then on the train and finally on the tram. I had rationed myself most strictly to one teaspoon of honey per day throughout that winter.

The honey was the last straw. I waited until Marie-Therese had gone to bed, then I went to the railway station. I queued for three hours and bought a ticket from Krakow to the Polish border.

When I got home Marie-Therese was still asleep. Very quietly I packed all her things in the travel bags, then I sat and waited. At about 6.00 in the morning I went and found a taxi. I gave the driver a thousand złoties and said he would have the same again, in addition to his fare, if he would wait outside my apartment block. He waited.

I rousted Marie-Therese from her sleep and told her to get dressed. I gave her a flask of tea and yesterday's loaf wrapped in newspaper. I took her bags downstairs. She followed. I opened the door to the taxi and she got in. We traveled in silence. At the station I handed her the train ticket.

- You'll be in Paris by early evening, I said.

I found her a seat beside the window in a nonsmoking compartment and, with the aid of a burly paratrooper, heaved her bags up onto the rack. The paratrooper grunted and sat down frowning thoughtfully as if someone had kicked him in a sensitive place.

I stood on the platform. Marie-Therese came to the window. She looked pale and disheveled in the yellow light. I had given her no time to comb her hair or wash. She stared down at me, face blank, eyes like currants in dough. She said quietly:

- You know, I don't fancy you no more. A terrible thing to say, but is true.

The train began to pull away. Over the noise of the engine she called:

- Maybe I send you chocolate.

I waved, she did not.

notebook

I have become a connoisseur of toilets. The prize for the worst - the absolute worst - goes to the hotel in Wambierzyce. The town is so small there is only one hotel, and the hotel is so small there is only one toilet. It was hot sticky August. I smelt the thing before I saw it, and then I heard it. The noise was that of hundreds of flies - great, fat, juicy, man-eating, shiny, black, east European flies. Stupefied by the heat and stench they strolled lazily along the walls, buzzed against the light bulb. The toilet floor was so deep in urine that some kind soul had actually placed two bricks for the user to perch on. The toilet bowl was heaped with a small mountain of shit and overflowing with piss and gamboling flies. It was not possible to flush the toilet as the water was cut off. Someone had plastered the walls to waist height with sculpted shit. My bowels simply seized up, refused to work. In a foul temper I went to the foyer of the hotel and demanded to see the manager and the hotel complaint book. The manager, with amused contempt, watched me write my comments, took the book, read what I had written, nodded, smiled and said:

- Yes. It's terrible, you know. In Poland toilets are our great national shame.

- Are you going to clean it?

He looked puzzled.

- Clean it? No. It's much too dirty for that...

At this point the woman in the tobacco kiosk asked me to move because, she said, I was blocking her display. She had her clients to consider, she said. I looked at the display: two packets of cigarettes and a bag of loose green tobacco. I moved.

*

Jan Sobieski's cavalry
Turns east again
And rides off
Wings beating[28]

In endless dreams
On Polish plains
Uhlans joust[29]
With grey hooded hordes

---

[28]King Jan Sobieski led the Allied cavalry into the rear of the Turkish forces at the battle of Vienna in 1683, ending the Turkish threat to western Europe but also removing the only threat to the rise of Muscovy. Polish cavalry at this time wore high feathered wings on their shoulders which, when they charged the enemy, made a terrifying noise.

[29]Uhlan from Polish *ułan* - lancer. Soviet Red Cavalry of the Polish-Soviet war of 1919-20 wore hooded caps.

Burning Worm

The poet Mickiewicz[30]
Queuing for toilet paper
Hastily rewriting his poem
'To my Muscovite Friends'

Slaughter in the
Morning air
A forest
Of burning bodies

*

When I lived in Wrocław I had a small studio-flat on the
top floor of an academic hostel. My room was 19/84,
which caused me no end of mirth. The hostel overlooked
Plac Grunwaldzki. This had once been an enormous
residential area, but in 1945 in the closing days of the war
it had been bulldozed flat by order of the Nazi Gauleiter to
make an air strip so that he and his cronies could fly out
of the besieged city to their Bavarian mountain bastion,
where they planned to make their final stand.[31]

Looking out from my building to the other side of the
square it was possible to see opposite a women's
university dormitory called the Girl of Twenty. In neon
strip lettering across the top of the building there was a
stirring motto: 'Youth, Beauty and Hope of Our town'. In
a way it was typical of the jingoism of western Poland.
You didn't see things like that in Warsaw. It was as if

---

[30]Reference to a poem, 'Muscovite Friends' by Adam
Mickiewicz [1798-1855], perhaps the greatest of the Polish
Romantic poets.

[31]Wrocław used to be the German city of Breslau, but was
reclaimed by Poland in 1945.

they were trying too hard. Except that during all the time I was there the neon lights never worked properly. Two of the letters had burned out so it now read *U..da* instead of *Uroda*, so the message was: 'Youth, Beauty and Thigh of Our Town.

One day my neighbours bought a small stereo record player. They invited me in to celebrate the purchase with wine and poppy-seed cake. They had tried the stereo out in the shop, but when they got it home only one speaker channel worked. Tadek found that if he placed his finger at a particular spot on the deck he could get both channels to work for a while. We sat around chatting and drinking and every so often Tadek would cock an ear, then place a finger on the deck. The conversation never paused. I asked Halina why they did not send the machine back to the factory. She laughed. Tadek called me a silly prick and asked if my time in Poland had taught me nothing.

- If we send it back to the factory it will get smashed up entirely. They won't repair it. They don't know how. They just assemble the parts. Half a stereo is better than none.

*

We are supposed to have a teachers' meeting, an important planning session to cover preparations for the next four intensive English courses and a revision programme for those students wanting to take the Proficiency or First Certificate exams in the summer. But almost everyone is late.

We sit around, waiting for the others, chatting with a visiting American Fullbright scholar here to teach American Literature. It is his first month in Poland and he is terribly depressed. Everyone he meets he accosts with the sentence:

- Hey, buddy, where can I send out for a pizza?

At a tea party in Konwiwium he tells me he had to cancel his seminar on *The Invisible Man* as none of his students had read the book. For him this is an enormous black mark against Polish students. They are lazy, uninterested, slack, lacking in fibre, and they have a nerve turning up to a seminar unprepared. The Poles are all far too polite with him. Nobody had read the book because nobody had been able to get hold of a copy. He reminds me of another American I met in 1976 in Wrocław. His name was Victor. He was a Chemist, also on a Fullbright. He spent his first nine months in Poland waiting for a simple glass condenser to make distilled water. Victor once said:

- This place really is in the stone age. Back home our computers are 13th or 14th generation. Here they are still only in the third generation.

This seemed like a bit of an exaggeration, but I did not know enough about computers to contradict him. I did know that students of 'Informatics' - computing by another name - often graduated without ever clapping eyes on a computer.

During a lull in the conversation Janina asked me about my boots. She wanted a pair like them for her husband. I said:

- They are new. I bought them yesterday...

- Are they warm?

- Yes, very warm. Look they have a fleece lining.

- Yeah? interrupts the Fullbright. Just so long as you don't expect me to admire them.

Janina changed the subject, saying she had seen students tearing down Solidarność posters in the market square. I ask if she is sure they were students. She says they looked like students, but that doesn't mean they really were students. She says:

- Maybe, if they were students, I can understand them. I mean, I hear people complaining about Solidarność on the buses and in the shops. And old people don't like Solidarność much at all. It seems to me that it is Solidarność that is causing the strikes now, and causing the shortages. I used to think it was the government, but now I don't.

- And if they were not students? If they were security agents?

- So it's a provocation. Another provocation. And I don't know what it means at all.

The only person missing by now was Ela. We waited. I noticed that the departmental secretary has moved her beauty spot. Usually it is placed just below and to the left of her mouth. But today the spot has moved away to inhabit territory above the lips. In the place where the beauty spot used to be there is now a large sore. She notices me looking and is embarrassed.

- Vitamin deficiency, she says. Ela, she says, also has an open sore on her neck, for the same reason, and she is pregnant.

At that moment the door burst open and Ela ran in. Instead of apologising she laid a parcel on my desk and quickly unwrapped it. She had bought a huge ham. It was beautifully cooked and peppered, and it lay there, in my office, on my desk. I felt dribble run down my chin. I clamped my mouth shut quickly and rubbed my beard with the back of my hand as if I had an itch. Ela said:

- The corner shop. There was no queue. I was the first. If you hurry…

Before I could say: But we are starting an important meeting, the room was empty. Just me. And the coat-rack, rocking gently back and forwards in the corner. Which meat shop had they gone to? On which corner? She had not said, but everyone seemed to know. If I could follow them I too could buy meat. But by the time I have locked up the office it is too late. I have no idea which way they have gone.

Slowly I went down the stairs and out of the building, to see where the university Solidarność posters had been torn down. A little old woman in a black widow's scarf stood reading a Solidarność notice board outside the main university building. She stood with her hands on her hips, slipped a piece of bread into her mouth, reading slowly, chewing with concentration. She turned, and waving an arm at the notice board, said to no-one in particular:

- These Solidarność types. Bastard worms, like all the rest. You'll see. It was never as bad as this even under Hitler. Then you could always buy a little ham or a slice of cheese. For them we are just blacks. Just blacks. If I was a slave they'd treat me better. I wish I was a slave. But I'm white and this is my country.

She spat, splashing my new boots with a gob of yellow phlegm, and waddled off, scattering the pigeons.

*

I went out to the countryside on a day trip. I stood in the open fields with a farmer. He paused from his work and leaned on an enormous scythe. He took a swig of tea from his flask and explained how the tanks had come racing through the village in 1939.

- The thing is, he said, wiping his forehead with a blue cloth cap and squinting into the dusty August sunlight. In these parts there is nothing to stop them. No mountains, see. And the rivers can all be forded or bridged. Of course it cuts both ways. The Germans went through here like a dose of salts, but five years later the Russians went through in the opposite direction just as quick.

Later we sat in the shade of his orchard eating sour little apples and drinking water from his well. His widowed sister, dressed completely in black sat with us for a while. She pumped icy water into the heat of day for me to wash. When I left she filled all my pockets with apples until I looked like a Michelin man. She bade me farewell in German:

- If you should want water again, or a chat, don't hesitate to come back…

*

One night I went to visit Margaret, a British lecturer in English literature, working for the British Council at Kraków University.[32] She lived above the Russian Institute and was always nervous that if there was trouble the Institute would be firebombed by the mob. She had a lovely little daughter, and the apartment always felt like a real home. It was lived in, with rugs askew, toys on the floor and books crammed higgledy piggledy onto the

---

[32]A little while after the visit recounted here, this lecturer, while on vacation in England, wrote an article for *The New Statesman* about what she had seen in Poland. As a result, she was advised not to return.

shelves. In the kitchen a Polish nanny was making soup and the smell wafted through the apartment. Nanny was mad that night, constantly muttering to herself, because Margaret allowed her daughter to sit on the ground, something no Polish mother would ever allow a girl child to do.

Margaret had invited me round because she had accumulated a pile of dissident literature and underground publications, items from Solidarność and the various factions within it. I was keen to see the stuff and if we pooled our very partial grasp of the Polish language we might understand more. Together we drank coffee and pored over pale carbon copies and badly duplicated pamphlets. All human life was there. Well, something for everybody at least. Poems by Milosz. A whole series of anti-Communist quotations from Kołakowski.[33] There was also a speech by inter-war leader General Piłsudski against Russian influence. There was also a life of Piłsudski, a review of evidence that the Russians were responsible for the Katyn massacre. I noticed a weird collection of messianic visions called *The Little Black Book of Poland* containing predictions made by a Polish hermit from visions provoked by the appointment of a Polish Pope in 1978. This volume also contained calculations designed to show exactly when the world will end. An article on 'Polish Political Worms'. Poems from Leszek Moczulski, stories, gossip, an anti-Semitic tract, directions on how to disable a soviet tank with a kilo of

---

[33]Leszek Kołakowski [b.1927]. The most outspoken of the Marxist revisionists, lecturer in philosophy at Warsaw University. Expelled from the Party 1966, sacked from his post at the university in the purge of 1968, moved to a professorship in Oxford 1969.

potatoes or a bucket of water. Instructions on how to make a Molotov cocktail - the author assumes there will still be petrol. A collection of traditional Polish recipes designed to restore the national kitchen to pre-communist standards, but for which the ingredients have been missing for over 30 years.[34]

Margaret and I pooled our knowledge of Polish to sift through them while nanny got Margaret's daughter ready for bed. Ola, one of Margaret's students arrived and she sat down with us to drink real [!] coffee and translate for us. As she did so, Ola grew more and more exasperated with us, and more appalled at our reading matter. Finally she decided it was time to go home. She drained her coffee cup, put on her coat and wound her scarf about her neck. Ola stood ready to leave, but with something to say.

- Why do you read this awful.... stuff? It's nonsense. All nonsense. This is the worst stuff around. And just because the people who wrote it are members of Solidarność, that does not mean that this is union policy. You should not judge Solidarność by this.

Margaret replied:

- OK. But this is just a random sample. And there is obviously a tremendous market for it. Even if it is rubbish. Even if the union is not responsible. People want it. They hunger for it. What can we say about that? Censorship has created a terrible hunger for garbage. The logic is that if a thing is banned then it must contain a truth the government doesn't want us to share. It looks

---

[34]Leszek Moczulski [b.1938], Catholic lyric poet, part of the generation of '68. Leader of the right-wing, nationalist, anti-Semitic KPN. His imprisonment in September 1980 transformed what had been a fringe group into a growing political force. [See also page 114.]

like real knowledge, a real restoration of meaning. It is popular. And that is part of what Solidarność has released, whether it wanted to or not. You have to ask what does the social movement represented by Solidarność actually contain. And you have to take that into account.

Ola was not pleased.

- And what will you say about us when you go home? That we hate Jews, that we have visions of the end of the world? It's not good.

She left and we read on...

*

Another kink in the rope,
It strains to stay straight
But another kink in the rope
And it turns it twists
It writhes like a
Burning worm
I am a hero
I resist
Summer rain
Heart singing
Far from death
Much nearer

- This worm in your poem, Maria said. Strange. No Pole would say such a thing. We would prefer to express a paradox. For us *robak* is a term of abuse. Do you think it is proper to refer to Poland as a worm?

- It is not Poland, necessarily. It is an expression of a state of mind: you, me, Kraków, Poland. All these things. Read it how you like.

- This Polish, maybe Irish, worm.... it prefers life underground, makes love with itself, eats dirt, lives in the dark.... hmm.... maybe you are right.

*

News on the radio tonight is that the Pope has issued a special blessing for everyone in Poland. Yippee! That should improve things. So why don't I feel any safer? Still I have a special blessing from the Pope.... that should make my parents happy.

piggy-wigg

One fine spring day I went out for a walk along the winding country lanes. The last of the winter snow still stood around in isolated dirty piles, but already there were buds on the trees, and if you turned your face to the sky you could feel the growing warmth of the sun. I amble on until I came across a farm cart with a huge pig in the back. It had run off the road and got a wheel stuck in a ditch. The driver, who smelt of home made fruit vodka, had just finished giving the horse a good thrashing with a birch twig. He said to me:

- Honoured sir, would you mind putting your shoulder here for a little minute.

He indicated a corner of the wagon. I nodded agreement and stood ready while he took the reins and gee'd up the horse. Between us the horse and I managed to get the wagon back on the road. I wiped mud from my hands and said:

- That's a fine looking pig. Have you just bought it?

- You're right, sir. A fine looking porker. But no. I've had him in the barn all winter, and now I'm taking him along the road for my friend to slaughter. We'll carve him into four.

It seemed indecent to discuss the pig's fate so openly with the beast standing near at hand. The driver looked thoughtful for a moment and said:

- You know this is the last pig in the whole valley? He made a sweeping gesture with his arm that imitated the horizon. The place was so flat you would not think of it as a valley at all. Yes, he said. Not another pig for miles.

- Don't you have piglets to rear for next year?

- No. Nothing. All gone.

- But what will you eat when the winter comes?

- Honoured sir, how should I know? In this country if you are a farmer, then you're an enemy of the people. I think there won't be any farmers by Christmas. What I grow this year I will keep for my own use, and the state can whistle. Maybe Solidarność can get us some pigs, but I doubt it. Ach! Why should I care? I'll get a job in a factory and then the state can feed me. Farming is a mug's game.

He thanked me for my help and whipped up the tired old horse.

- Come and see me next week. The house behind the post office. I'll have some pork sausage with garlic for you.

And off he went, cursing the ancestry of his horse, with the pig oinking and farting, flapping its ears and blinking in the sunlight.

Burning Worm

*

While I was wandering around I met a Gypsy woman. My first encounter with Polish Gypsies had not been edifying. When I refused to give a beggar woman money 'to buy milk for the children' she took me by the arm and shouted:
- May a ball of fire fly up your mother's cunt!.
The standard reply, I was later told, was: 'Prick of a donkey up your mother's arse'.

Perhaps it was just as well I didn't know that, because this woman was different. She was in her late forties, I guess. She wore the usual headscarf, multi-layered skirts and brightly coloured anorak, and she had a gold tooth. She did not beg, but spoke quietly to me in Romany. When she realised I was not a Gypsy she apologised and, in Polish, offered to read the cards for me.

It was very pleasant to sit in the apartment with the kids falling around on the floor and the smell of fresh tea. The men folk piled their guitars, double bass and accordion in the corner, drank tea and smoked in the next room, still wearing their brightly coloured anoraks. She chased the kids out of the room. They kicked off their shoes and stood barefoot in the doorway, watching. She clicked tarot cards flat on the table, thought for a while and then said:
- You will have had trouble with the milicja. They will come to your home again, soon, but nothing bad will happen. You will be very ill next month and for a little while after, but it will soon pass. You will never have children, but you will marry. You will have problems finding love for a long time to come. First you will meet a girl who won't love you, but will pretend that she does, this will give you great anguish. Also a girl will become

pregnant and she will blame you - don't be fooled, you will not be the father. You will meet the girl you are going to marry in a few days time, but you won't marry her for a long, long time, more than ten years. When you get back to your flat there will be a parcel waiting for you - a food parcel maybe. It is from your mother.

We drank more tea.

- You didn't run away, and you didn't curse me.
- Why should I?
- Poles do.
- They don't trust foreigners.
- But we've been here for years. Hundreds of years.
- Still, you don't look like Poles.
- We are not Poles, so why should we. Anyway neither do you.
- No, I look like a Romany.

She laughed.

- I was sure you were Rom. Something about you.... Some of our people are very pale. It happens. You are a foreigner...
- Everywhere.
- It shows.

I offered her money for the reading. With a quick glance into the back room she shook her head in refusal. I stepped into the back room and shook hands with all the men in turn. They were very wary. At the door she would not shake hands. It was not allowed for a woman to shake hands with a man. It was the moment in a film when someone says something profound. But neither of us spoke. She waved awkwardly as I left.

As things turned out, it was a very accurate reading. When I got home there was a note from the post office in my door. I collected a food parcel from my mother. A few days later I met Maria at an alcohol free party. Our fingers touched over a bowl of breadsticks. I walked Maria home and she gave me her phone number. That night, while I was at the party, the milicja searched my apartment again.

*

In May the weather was gentle and the skies were blue. When the buds were still bursting on the trees and the mud had dried underfoot, I went on a photographic spree round the old Jewish quarter of Kazimierz. I made for the market, ambling down side streets, snapping old and derelict buildings, the ruined synagogues, whatever took my fancy. It was wonderful to be able to wander about without a heavy overcoat and gloves, wonderful to feel warm breezes against my face. The smell of fresh bread hung in the air.

The market place was busy. Local farmers had brought meat and eggs to sell, knowing that the winter had driven prices on the open market sky-high. Although there were lots of people milling back and forth, the stalls were not in fact doing much business. I wandered on, hoping that the Jewish cemetery might be open. Some of the tombs were spectacular and I wanted to take pictures. However, just before the gate to the cemetery there was a man on a soap box. On either side of him two men held a banner aloft which read: 'Grunwald Patriotic Union - The Jews are our misfortune'.[35] I stopped to listen.

---

[35]Grunwald Patriotic Union, a shady Party front organisation connected to Mieczyslaw Moczar and ZBoWiD, the brawling anti-Semitic organisation for wartime partisans.

- The hooky-nosed bastards are in league with their cousins in Moscow and on Wall Street, and with the Mafia. And they want to destroy us. They are everywhere and we must root them out. Those bastards in KOR[36] don't fool us. They are not the friends of Polish workers. They are Jews leading us to destruction. Why else do you think that Jews like Mazowiecki, Michnik, Kuroń would change their names? They are in disguise. They want to appear as good Poles.... And don't think they are confined to KOR. They are everywhere. In the government there are some very suspicious characters. Look at Deputy Premier Jagielski, he's another one. Don't be fooled by his charm....

Just across the square from the meeting there was an electrical goods store. A whole family of farmers arrived on their horse and wagon and they bought an enormous fridge freezer. The family helped to carry this huge white chest down the steps and load it onto the wagon. Then the family toasted each other in vodka and climbed aboard. Sitting atop the freezer they gee'd up the horse and trotted off. That is an image of Poland. A miracle of modern science and engineering going home on a horse drawn cart. Poland: nose in the 20th century, arse in the 18th century.

picnic

At the end of May teaching virtually ceased as the university sank itself into preparation for exams. We had our last crammer classes for the English Proficiency exams. For this we went back to Janowice. I felt I had

---

[36]KOR: see page 106.

spent more than half the year in this village, and when I totted up the days it was certainly a substantial part of the winter months.

It was agreed right at the start that we would hold a party on the last night, but preparations started early. A group of men went off to the surrounding villages to see if they could scavenge some food, another group went off along the main road in a car to see if they could find any alcohol - I didn't like to tell them they could go straight to the house of the Parish priest in case it gave them the wrong idea. The women went off to gather branches for a bonfire and to make a clearing where we could eat, drink, sing and even dance if we felt like it.

Beside the woods was a lake, alive and noisy with thousands of frogs. The woods hummed with birds and insects. We built a bonfire of dry wood with a stack of damp wood nearby in reserve, and then we sat around soaking up the sunlight that filtered through the trees.

Along the woodland path the food gathering party returned in triumph. They had a huge sack of potatoes and seven kilos of sausage. We asked how they had managed to find the elusive sausage, but they just laughed, winked and whispered:

- The usual ways, bribery, contacts.

They were so pleased with their foray that one of the men presented a psychologist called Basia with a crown of spring flowers, then they carried her shoulder high round the lake. She was absolutely delighted with their attention, but they stopped at a corner of the pond that was thick and scummy with frog-spawn and said that they had to throw her in because the Great Frog God demanded a sacrifice. Basia protested, but the men explained that the god needed a virgin to appease him. Her shrieks were most gratifying.

Watching proceedings from a distance was Marek, an astrophysicist who specialised in weighing stars, but who told me in confidence that he was really much more interested in the search for black holes. He laughed at the sacrifice at the lake edge and said:

- You know, if the Great Frog God needed a virgin, this offering would give him terrible indigestion.

Marek, like most of the eligible males had suffered in Basia's games. She had a habit of getting close to men, physically and mentally. She used discos and socials to press herself against the men of her choice, would lead men to one side and engage them in ernest conversation staring deep into their faces. She led them to believe that she would support them in their ventures, that she had lusted after their mind and body for months on end, that all she needed was the opportunity. Our courses - out in the country - were a perfect setting, and it was there that the men arrived, all of a lather, primed for the encounter. And it was there that Basia deserted them - or rather, it was there that she ignored them completely.

I half expected that the men really would throw her into the lake, but they did not. The alcohol foraging party returned just in time to save her. In those first warm spring days the wounds of winter heal quickly. Several of the men might have considered throwing her in, but in the end they were Polish gentlemen. I don't think anybody really cared that day. We were all desperate to have a good time.

That night we sat out in the open air. We were rich. We had 100 bottles of beer between forty people. It was the first alcohol most of us had tasted for more than eight months and the effect was instantaneous: from the moment the party started we all seemed to walk with a careful footfall, and a slightly dazed expression. Bill, an American teacher said:

- Whoopee! We're all gonna get shit-faced...

The bonfire grew to a magnificent roaring beacon. We roasted the sausages on sticks, trying to keep ourselves out of the smoke. The grease dropped into the fire and added to the roar, or it rolled up our hands, along our wrists and sank into our sleeves and cuffs.

The potatoes were rotten. We split them and roasted those that were edible. Somehow it didn't really matter. We lay on our backs and let the beer and sausage gurgle about inside while Marek the astronomer named parts of the clear, star-packed sky for us.

Bill told us about a book he and his wife were translating.[37] They were having a difficult time persuading western publishers to take a project about Poland seriously. We chatted on about American politics, and then about poetry. After a while Marek explained to us how he set about weighing stars. Somebody - a disembodied voice in the darkness said:

- Will they come, the Russians.

Someone else replied:

- Why would they? It's a hopeless situation for the military.
- For the Russians, yes, said another voice. But it's our own military we have to watch out for.
- Yes?
- They are everywhere, checking, prying, testing.

---

[37]Almost certainly William Brand, who later, with his wife, translated the works of Ryszard Kapuscinski into English

- Don't talk such nonsense. Our soldiers? They are pledged to protect us. Remember the oath of allegiance?

Someone addressed me directly.

- What do you think will happen?

- I have no idea, but I've heard there will be a military coup in September. A milicja-man told me they have already cleared the jails of 23,000 petty criminals.

- Yes I've heard that too, said a voice on the other side of the fire.

- Oh Lord what will become of us? said a woman behind me.

Bill stood up - he was about 6 foot 4 inches and big across the shoulders. He was wielding a wooden club. Poised at the edge of the firelight he said:

- Toss me one of them taters.

I threw a potato. With a ripple of the shoulders he hit it into the darkness. We listened. There was a splash from the lake. The frogs fell silent. Bill said:

- Keep 'em coming.

Swinging away like one of the baseball heroes of yesteryear, Bill sent potatoes sailing into the night sky. There was a rhythm to it: a whack, a pause, then a distant thud or splash. It seemed like an age before the spuds landed and I wondered if he had hit them into orbit. Eventually Bill tired and sat down with the rest of us, brooding on the edge of the firelit circle.

I looked around. Barbara had snuggled up to Marek. Maria had fallen asleep on my shoulder. Her mouth was open and she was dribbling on my sleeve. After a while, Bill stood, tossed a few more potatoes into the air and dispatched them into the darkness, then sat again staring into the flames. It was an odd night. Forty people, some of them Poland's leading intellectuals, up to their elbows in grease, all slightly drunk discussing the weight of stars, listening for the sound of a distant crash.

andrzej d.: polish poet

I met Andrzej through his girlfriend Ela. This was just a few months after I arrived in Poland on my first visit. Probably in 1976. She invited me for a meal at her parents' flat in the crumbling district of Wrzeszcz in Gdańsk. Over rye soup Andrzej said: 'So, you've been in Poland how long.... ? Let's see what you've learned. Name for me three Polish rivers. Repeat for me the opening lines of the Polish National Anthem. Name any three Polish generals - and I don't mean Communists. What was the Confederation of Targowica? What is significant about the date May 3rd? What was....?' The quiz went on for some time.

He was a squat, muscular character with fashionably long hair, a droopy mustache; he chain smoked *Sports*, the cheapest and roughest of Polish cigarettes. Over sausage, fried onions and rye bread he asked me which Polish writers I liked. 'Herbert, Lem, Mrożek.... a strange combination. What about the classics? Or are they too Polish for you?' I didn't know whether to be flattered or flustered by his questioning.

He took it upon himself to keep the company's glasses filled. When the vodka ran out he produced a bottle of 'Polski Dżin' from his briefcase. The candle on the table spluttered to a finish and he replaced it muttering that the flame must dance to show that the spirit still lived around the humble board. After spiced apple cake he took out a sheaf of his verses and gave a passionate, intense reading.

Ela's mother and father came in to listen. They stood by the doorway. Ela's mother, a doctor, is very deaf and kept whispering loudly: 'What was that? What did he say?' Her father, who is a lawyer, said that Andrzej was a tremendous nincompoop whose knowledge of Polish history was derived from CIA propaganda broadcasts on Radio Free Europe. But nevertheless, her father added, he is obviously a very talented poet.

Yes Andrzej was a poet - or as he would say, a PO-ET: earnest, deeply patriotic, massively cynical about the achievements of Polish Socialism and bitterly contemptuous of all things Russian. So far his poems had not achieved any kind of publication - official or underground. Ela had great faith in him though, and she would spend hours typing out copies with tired old carbons so that Andrzej would have poems to hand out at parties and meetings.

After that first encounter I met Andrzej several times. I might have passed my Polish Test, but he made it clear that he still regarded me as a *frajer* - a monk, an innocent.[38] Once I watched him engrave the word KATYN on the wall of a public lavatory. While he carved he explained that Katyn was the place where the NKVD[39] had murdered 15,000 Polish officers and then tried to pretend the Nazis had done it. Mostly we talked about the ghetto

---

[38]Hinks makes mistaken use of a Polish idiom here. 'Frajer', a loan word from English 'friar', is GULAG slang. It means a mafia gang leader, a big fish. The connection with the idea of the monk is that both enjoy protection. An innocent would have been a 'musul-man'. Hinks has misunderstood Andrzej's contempt for him. Andrzej clearly suspected that Hinks was a secret milicja informer rather than an innocent.

[39]NKVD: People's Commissariat for Internal Affairs: Soviet Secret Police.

mentality of much Polish literature, for and against; about why Polish literature had never become a world literature; about whether, if Polish literature had not become so ghettoised, would it still have remained 'Polish'. One day while we were sitting in a bar sipping beer he said: 'You mustn't think of Gdańsk as Poland. It's an old German city we took over at the end of the war. If you want to see the real Poland you must go to Krakow. Or better still, go to Lwów or Wilno - towns the Russians stole from us.'

Ela and I translated a batch of his poems into English. We circulated them to about a dozen British Poetry magazines, but without any success. To be a dissident in those days it was necessary to be a Russian or a Czech. It also helped if you were visibly harassed, exiled, arrested, sent to a labour camp, beaten up, kept under surveillance or any combination of the above. The subtleties of Polish dissidence had yet to be charted, the damage of being neither published nor censored had yet to be imagined. This was, after all, some time before the rise of Solidarność made Poland briefly fashionable.

But Andrzej was alone, even among dissidents. He tried hard. He stood outside the gates of the giant Lenin shipyard distributing verses, typed by Ela, to the shipyard workers as they came off shift. They took the proffered sheets with a puzzled but polite air. Since the demonstrations of 1968, students and intellectuals had been given a grudging acceptance by the workers. The demonstrations that brought about the downfall of Gomułka in 1970[40], and the events in Radom in 1976[41]

---

[40]Władysław Gomułka, First Secretary of the Polish Communist Party, came to power with the 'thaw' of 1956 but soon proved a disappointment. On 12 December 1970 steep price increases were announced. Two days later angry crowds

were to bring them even closer. But Poetry at the shipyard gates? Well maybe. Give it a try. Give the lad a chance. You never know. They carried the verses off, but when the blue and yellow coastal trains arrived in the nearby port of Gdynia or in Sopot, or at their destinations in the wet sand lands of Kaszubia, the poems had already been found out. Too wry. Too allusive, even by Polish standards. I found several copies of the poems on the bench seat of the local train on my way to work in the morning and quietly returned them to Ela.

---

in Gdańsk set Party headquarters on fire and the milicja opened fire on the crowd. In the towns of Gdynia, Elbląg, Słupsk and Szczecin shipyard workers and others went on strike. In Gdynia the milicja and army, mistaking crowds of people returning to work for massed ranks of saboteurs, opened fire. Almost certainly Gomułka had given the order to fire, but in the recriminations which followed Gomulka was blinded by a stroke and was ousted from the leadership.

[41]Radom, a town in central Poland. There, in June 1976, against a backdrop of protest at changes to the constitution, crowds demonstrated against yet another attempt to raise meat prices. Protesters raided the Party HQ canteen and then, so the milicja said, went on a looting spree in which four people died, seventy-five were injured and over $1,000,000 worth of damage was done. The milicja took brutal reprisals. They arrested and beat over 2000 people, including workers from the Ursus tractor factory who were also sacked from their jobs and kicked out of their accommodation. Special summary courts sentenced hundreds more to jail terms. KOR [Committee Defending Workers] grew out of the attempt by a small group of intellectuals to defend workers from Radom and Ursus against victimisation by the milicja and the courts. KOR grew steadily over the next few years to become a political pressure group, well known to the milicja and to shipyard activists like Lech Wałęsa. [See also page 106.]

If it was martyrdom he was after - and I suspect that martyrdom would have made his life much simpler - then martyrdom did not come.

They say that three militiamen are needed to make an arrest. One to read, one to write and one to keep an eye on the other two dangerous intellectuals. But when Andrzej encountered the milicja they always seemed to be in pairs. Andrzej was stopped and questioned. They thought that he was distributing literature for the illegal Free Trades Union of the Coast, a forerunner of Solidarność that was getting started at around that time. But when they realised that he was a poet they let him go without even glancing at his verses. When he was stopped the second time, a high ranking officer interviewed him and then let him go with a warning about littering.

Andrzej did eventually get arrested. He was declaiming his verse sat astride the cannon of a Russian T34 tank used as a monument to the Russian war-dead, parked just opposite the students club. Alcohol was forbidden in the club, but a bottle of vodka was usually circulating under the counter. Andrzej was not arrested for his verses but for his drunkenness - not a simple offence in Poland. Treatment of drunks was so severe, and the consequences so prolonged, that most milicjants operated an unwritten rule: if a drunk could walk, then walk he should; but if he fell over, or could not progress under his own steam, then arrest was inevitable. I doubt if the milicja would have been able to make out much from Andrzej's poetry reading, but still, they could have done him for desecrating a war memorial or even inciting anti-Russian feeling. They thought they were being kind. They only arrested him when he fell off the tank.

Burning Worm

He was taken to a special milicja medical unit in Wrzeszcz. He was stripped, hosed down with cold water, dried off, put to bed on a wooden board, hosed down a second time in the morning and then escorted home. He was expected to pay the cost of his 'accommodation', he was fined - without appeal - for antisocial behaviour. Furthermore, there was a black mark against his name that detracted an exact number of points from his end of term exams at the university.

I think this was some kind of turning point for Andrzej. He became very quiet and withdrawn. At first he tried to study hard to make up for the black mark, but then he abandoned his efforts and decided to try and repeat the year by falling ill. I heard that he was trying to buy a medical certificate. He need not have bothered. Within a very short time his drinking caused ulcerated legs. The ulcers refused to heal. They were so bad that he failed his medical for conscription into the army and attained a medical classification so low that it was unheard of among his contemporaries. We joked that in time of war his function would be that of non returnable hostage.

I met Ela and Andrzej at a party some months after his army medical. Andrzej would not show his poems, nor would he read them for us. He was still taking tablets for his legs, but had not stopped drinking. He had heard, presumably through Ela, that I wanted to research a book about Gdańsk and the German novelist Günter Grass - Grass had lived in the city when it was still called Danzig, in an apartment block just around the corner from where Ela now lived. Andrzej said: 'So you are leaving us for England. And what will you teach your students there about us Poles? Will you teach them about Grass?' No, I replied. I don't think there would be enough interest in the

subject to do that. 'But why not?' he said. 'Why not do it
if you are free to do it? In the West you are Free, yes?'
Yes, I said. In a way we are free. In Poland the censor
says what you can or cannot do, and that creates a hunger
for what the censor refused to pass, whether it's any good
or not. What is approved by the censor is often by
definition of little real interest to the Polish public. In the
West we have The Market. The Market censors us
through our stomachs and through the pockets of
would-be publishers. We cannot do what we cannot sell.
If there is no market for a thing, a book say, then the
chances are that it will not get written. And if someone
should write it, that it will not get published, and if it is
published that it will not sell. That is not to say that it is a
bad book.... Andrzej snorted in disbelief. 'Don't give me
that Communist propaganda! Free is Free!' Ela did her
best to cover up his anger. Later she returned to apologise.
'You must forgive my Andrzej.... he is.... well.... a poet'.
There was a hint that Ela's apology for her boyfriend was
also an apology for her connection with him.

I forgive poets least of all. It was clear to me that this
was not the Andrzej who had written:

> In Poland the rain falls
> In America you press a button
> And the rain stops.

But perhaps it was the same man. Perhaps he was right.
Perhaps I was a *frajer*. Maybe I had mistaken naive belief
for subtle irony.

I did not see Andrzej again for about four years.
During that time he and Ela had split up. He failed to get
his degree. He still produced a poem from time to time,

but ever more infrequently it seemed. He preferred going out with his pals. He had started work in one of the offices at the Lenin shipyard. His hair was almost gone, his face was pudgy, his body was swollen. He wheezed. Małgosia, who worked with him for a while, said that he took a bottle of vodka to work in his briefcase instead of sandwiches.

Four years later, I caught a glimpse of Andrzej. I had thought he would surely be among the first to put his dissident anger at the service of Solidarność, especially since he worked in the shipyard. But no. For him Solidarność was too slow, other dissidents were too cautious. He suspected that they were all feathering their own nests; too many people were 'on the take' both in the Party and in the Union; too many deals were being done in private; too many empires were being built. His cynicism had become unbounded, the borders of common sense had been demolished. The government was filled with Jews, the Party was run by Jews, the Union was advised by Jews. If the Jews didn't get you one way, then they got you another. The Jews had the West all sewn-up too, and that, he said, was why the Pope was so slow to help Poland. When I asked him if he was still writing he said, 'Yes'. Then after a moment's thought he said, 'No.... Who would I write for?'

I have not seen Andrzej since then. Małgosia, an infallible source of information about her contemporaries in Gdańsk, tells me that Ela has wiped Andrzej from her history altogether, has almost no memory of him. Małgosia also says that when Martial Law was declared Andrzej applied to become a censor, but she cannot tell me if he was successful or not.

Burning Worm

visa

Every so often foreigners have to go to milicja Headquarters to renew their work and residence permit. It is a tedious and time wasting business, but the bureaucracy must have something to do, the ritual must be honoured. And what makes it even more irritating is that a contract of employment does not necessarily coincide with the duration of the work permit.

I went to Kraków milicja HQ, told the policewoman at the desk that my contract had been extended and that as a result I wanted to renew my visa and work permit. She, bored and bad tempered, ushered me into a waiting room full of similar supplicants. In spite of the tobacco shortage a dense blue fog hung over the room. I felt I had stepped onto the Somme battlefield in that moment of tense, living silence just after the artillery had ceased fire before the infantry went over the top. There was that same air of resignation, bloody mindedness, simmering resentment, residual fear that war veterans exude.

We sat. And sat. And sat some more. Every so often - about once every hour - the door would open and one of us would be called in to interview. There were no more seats in the waiting room and outside in the corridor a queue had formed, stretching along the corridor through the front door, down the steps and out onto the snow covered street.

Eventually something roughly approximating to my name was called and with weary bones and an aching bum I stirred myself into the interview room. An impeccably uniformed major sat at a glass topped desk, a glass of lemon tea at his elbow. His English was excellent.

- Good afternoon. How may I help you?

- Good afternoon. I would like to renew my visa.

- Renew? How renew?

- Well my visa expires soon and I would like to renew it.

- You mean you want to extend your tourist visa?

- No. I mean my work visa.... I work here at the university.

- You work here? In Poland?

- That's right.

- Impossible. He made a flicking gesture with his wrist as if to dismiss the notion. 'I am head of this department. We deal with all foreign workers. No foreigner works in this city without a personal interview by me. You understand? I interview all foreigners. Me. Personally.

- Look, I said. And I opened my passport to show him the stamp of my entry visa and the little buff card of the work visa.

He took the visa and turned at once to his filing cabinet riffling through the files hastily.

- But I have.... nothing under your name.... yet you have a visa...

There was a long pause. He ran his hand through his hair.

- Well, security might have borrowed the file, but they are supposed to.... to leave a docket.

He sat down again, leaned back in his chair and regained a little of his composure.

- You have been here before, I believe.

- That's right.

- And how long do you plan to stay?

- I have a job at the university, so at least a year.

- A job. I see. And how long have you been here?

- A year.

- No, I mean when did you arrive, this time?

171

- On this visa? Yes, a year ago. But I was here for a while before that, on another visa.

- A year....? He kicked the desk in panic. My God! A year? A whole year....?

- Yes, see, the date of my arrival is stamped in my passport.

- I don't believe it! This is absolutely impossible!

- Look, I'm sorry, I said. I really must get back to my office. I've lost almost a whole day here....

- I don't think you understand the seriousness of the case. If I don't have a file on you, if I don't have any record of a visa, then there is every possibility that the your visa is a forgery, and if it is a forgery, then it is possible that you are a spy.... or something.

- But I got the visa right here from this office. Look at the stamp, look at the signatures.

- Forgeries. All forged.

- To what purpose?

- How should I know? Western agents are trying a thousand different ways to get to Solidarność

- Just a moment, I work for the British Council, which is part of the British Diplomatic Service. My appointment was approved by the Ministry of Education in Warsaw. I'm here under an arrangement drafted by First Secretary Edward Gierek himself. My papers are in order. It is yours that will not stand scrutiny.... If I was living here on forged documents I would not need to come to you to renew my visa. I would already have a forged renewal.

There was a long silence.

- This is very bad. Very bad. You have been here a whole year without my knowledge, with no file, no record...

- Perhaps you were on holiday, I said. Perhaps one of your deputies, someone unfamiliar with the system...

His eyes lit up.

- The signature on the visa! Of course! He snatched the visa, stared at it intently, then he threw it down on the desk.

- Damn it! Illegible!

He paced the room for a moment, his boot-heels biting into the polished wooden floor. Then he picked up the phone and snarled an order. After a moment a tall blond militia-woman entered. He yelled at her:

- Which son of a bitch was my deputy while I was on my summer vacation?

She blushed, thought for a moment and then said:

- Lieutenant Zalewski.

- Zalewski, you marinated prick! Get in here. Now!

Lieutenant Zalewski stood at attention just inside the door.

- Zalewski, when did you take over the issue of visas?

- Sir?

- There's a chap here who has been living in Poland for a year and we have no record of him. Can you explain that?

- You mean.... that I.... ? The Lieutenant stepped forward and picked up the visa. He looked at it for a moment and then his brow cleared.

- Sir, I acted as your deputy while you were on vacation. We can check in the office diary. The date stamp on this visa shows that it was issued after you had resumed your post, sir.

There was a long silence.

- Well if I didn't issue it, and you didn't issue it, where did it come from?

All three swiveled to stare at me.

They told me to go away. I did. A few days later I received a summons to return to milicja HQ for a second interview. I arrived on time, was ushered past the waiting horde, to the inner office. There was no sign of the major from the previous interview. A new major sat behind the desk. He fixed a cigarette into an amber holder and spoke very slowly and carefully.

- I think it is best if we begin from the beginning, as if this was a new visa application, and forget all about the previous.... confusion.

I nodded. He slid a long questionnaire over the desk towards me. Name. Place of work in Poland. Polish address. Address in Britain. National origin. Polish family connections. Education. Party membership. Social class.

This last question had me confused.

- I'm not sure how to answer this, I said.

- Well, we are interested in your social standing in Britain. Now, let's see.... you finished University? Well then, you are intelligentsia.

- Doesn't that mean I work with my brain? That I am employed to.... well, think?

- Yes. It means that you come from the educated classes. From the intellectuals. That you aspire to that part of the nation which exercises independent thought as part of its profession.

- I see. But in my case this is not true.

- What work did you do in England?

- I was a lavatory attendant...

- What? But you have a university degree!

- I couldn't find work. The free market, you know? There was no work for my qualifications. Teaching in Poland is my first real job.

The major looked serious.

- So you are a victim of capitalist economics.

- Aren't we all?

- But put it another way, he mused. Our fine young Polish students, the cream of the nation, are taught by British lavatory cleaners. Hmm.... I don't think we should pursue that. Very well, what about the social origins of your family? Your father, for example, he was a shopkeeper, a businessman, a banker, he employed how many workers in his factory? So, we can write bourgeois...

- My father drives a van for the Post Office.

- A worker? A proletarian?

- Yes.

- And his son went to university?

- It's a bourgeois strategy - extract the best minds from working class, absorb them into the middle classes.

- What about your grandfather?

- A tram conductor.

- Grandmother?

- A typist.

- Bothers? Sisters?

- My brothers work in the Post Office, a shop and in a car factory. My sister works in a restaurant...

- Shit. OK, enough, enough. Just write 'Proletarian', and let Warsaw worry about it, eh?

I wrote Proletarian.

- So! What kind of car do you drive? Cadillac? Mercedes? Volkswagen?

- No car. Can't afford it.

- Do you have a fine big house with many rooms and a garden?

- I rent a room.

- Do you smoke? Marlborough, Benson & Hedges.... what?

- I don't smoke.

- You joke?
- No smoke, no joke.

The major chewed the end of his pencil for a moment. He was quite distressed by his thoughts. Very slowly he opened a desk draw, took out a bottle of vodka and two glasses. He filled the glasses.

- No house. No car. No job.... Capitalism is not the enemy it once was.... Do you like Polish girls.
- Of course.
- Well, my advice is: drink and fuck. There is nothing else for foreigners to do here anyway. He gestured at my papers on the desk. But you have been here a year already, so you know that.
- And alcohol is banned, I said.

He laughed and raised his glass.

- Yes.... By order of Solidarność alcohol is banned.

The two of us sat there, frowning at the official forms that lay between us, drinking.

maria

Tadek, one of my mature students, turned up at my flat. He was wearing full combat overalls and camouflage netting on his steel helmet. He held the helmet in his hands, playing with the netting. On his head he wore the maroon beret of the paratroopers. He apologised and said he would not be able to attend that last few classes of this term because he had been called up for summer maneuvers. I knew Tadek as a chemistry teacher. He was also a lieutenant in the army reserve and has charge of a chemical warfare platoon. His dual identity disturbed me more than it did him. When he explained about the maneuvers he laughed:

- Probably we're preparing for the coup.

Everybody knew about the coup except Solidarność.

He kissed Maria's hand with a military gallantry that irked her. When he had gone she said:

- I know him from the university. He is stupid. A little boy playing at soldiers.

From my balcony I watched him walk across the children's playground. He jumped the chalked hopscotch marks, his shambling teacher's gait already transformed into the steely stride of the paratrooper.

By this time there were mixed patrols of the army and the milicja on the streets. The soldiers carried rifles with fixed bayonets, and automatics. The milicja did not want to be associated with the army, and often they would patrol down opposite sides of the same street at the same pace. When the army paused, the milicja would stand on the opposite corner, waiting. Usually the army patrols were made up of paratroopers, but at the end of September the paratroopers disappeared and different troops took their place. The newcomers were from an armoured division based near Warsaw. They wore black berets and sometimes black baggy overalls. Usually they did not carry rifles or automatics, but made do with a pistol strapped to their leg, cowboy fashion.

I mentioned this change to Maria, but she assured me it meant nothing. But I was determined to make some sense of it. I spent two days talking with ordinary local Solidarność members, trying to build up some picture of what they wanted from the union. There was a sharp divide between male and female membership. The women were not keen on acts of heroism, and preferred improvements in daily life, food supplies, etc. But the men were involved in a bluff act of machismo and seemed ready for conflict over matters of principle. The women were reluctant to become involved in the running of the union, and who could blame them for that. They said they had responsibilities the men simply wouldn't take over: shopping, standing in queues, housework, cooking. But it seemed to me that women were reluctant to become active members of the union in the sense of initiating discussion or making use of the democratic structures available to them, even in ordinary meetings at the workplace. Also, the Solidarność decision to create an electoral college at the top of the union, in order to arrange appointments to key union posts, also represented a general refusal to take decisions. Perhaps this is a feeling which was understandable after so many years of the Party taking all decisions for everyone. For the men it was only slightly different. They too would have liked someone to take control, make decisions. They liked to advise, criticise, caucus, conspire, oppose, plot and politic. But they too did not like to lead, to be responsible. And many saw the union simply as a way of advancing their career outside the crippling stasis of Party influence. This struck me as the real achievement of the Party - a mixture of conservatism and opportunism, both inside its own ranks and outside, in the ranks of the union. So much for socialist achievements.

Again I mentioned my worries about what underpinned the union, to Maria. I chose a bad day. The leaders of her office Solidarność circle had just imposed a financial levy without consulting the membership. She looked at me as if I were some kind of an idiot:

- Has it taken you so long to realise these things? Something you must know about Poles is that they will talk about principles, morality and freedom all day long - all day! But they know nothing of these things, and they don't want to know because these things bring with them all kinds of responsibilities. All they know about is themselves. Self interest. All they care about is number one. Solidarność opens up a career for them, for all those who could not make it into the party, for all those who could not make it any further in the Party, for all those who think that the Party might just be finished - all those people who deprived Poland of their best efforts for years. They are opportunists, that is all. All of them. When the military move against them - and I hope they do it soon - only a handful of these Solidarność people will resist. Mostly they will all go back to work and carry on just as before, drinking and shirking. Only then it will be worse because they will all claim to be martyrs, and in their eyes they will have good reason to behave just as they have always done. Whatever we do it is always a mess....

Once I asked her why she was not enthusiastic about Solidarność. She was a reluctant member of the union and found herself between Solidarność and the Party - neither of which was acceptable or trustworthy. For her Solidarność was the product of the Party, its mirror image. She said:

- I simply can't believe why so many people, people who I thought were very nice, suddenly want to join this union. They never showed any interest in this kind of thing before. Did they join the opposition in the 1970s? No. Did they help workers in any way? No. Why should they? The workers had no power then. But now it is different. They all pretend to support the workers, but really they are just protecting their own backsides in case the workers win. I just don't trust these people. They set one group of Poles against another. Don't think for one minute that Poland is a classless society, or that it is a one class society. It is a peasant society, but some of the peasants work in factories. But I am a teacher, a member of the tiny middle class, and it is against me and people like me that Solidarność will take its revenge for the privileges we are supposed to enjoy under communism. When I finish my doctorate I will earn less than a labourer in the shipyard. But when they get a pay rise you can be sure it will come out of my pocket. When they rise up and take power, they will rise up against me. Me. Directly me...

Her friends called her *stara czerwona* but her relationship with her father undercut this description.[42] She was more complicated. Her father was a Party member: honest, loyal, incorruptible. He was an accountant with a local firm, but lost his job when Solidarność threatened to strike unless all Party members were removed from the firm. He had never made a penny from his membership of the Party or the 'high protection' it offered him. He was a quiet man who at first believed everything the Party told him and then later was one of the first to admit that the Party had a huge corrupt element within its ranks, and that it made terrible mistakes in planning and appointments to high office.

- Nevertheless, he would say, given Poland's geopolitical reality and the problems of social re-organisation.... the Party is the only organisation with the power to do anything in Poland, and therefore is the proper place for debate, and the only true initiator of social renewal. Solidarność is an outburst of justified moral protest and

---

[42]Literally 'old red'.

unless the Party and the bureaucracy listen to it and find a way to cooperate with it, Solidarność will be forced to become a political movement with ambitions to govern. And that will mean real trouble.

Maria's opinion of her father is that he is a mug, a simpleton, a sucker. I did not think that Maria had a true grasp of her father's experience, but that was between father and daughter, so I kept my own council. One night he showed me several Party documents, including the Party's plans for economic renewal. The Party and the Union, Maria and her father, they all argue like Jacob and the Angel: I'll let go your throat if you stop beating me. No I'll stop beating you if you let go my throat. Later I overhead him telling Maria that I was receiving a negative picture of Solidarność from her and that she should be more careful to present a balanced view:

- He sees this country through your eyes, he said.

She replied:

- He has been here for years already. He has his own experiences and his own opinions. He makes up his own mind. It is not me.

Maria asked why I had come to Poland. I explained that I had been unemployed for a long time, that I had only ever managed to get part-time teaching - a week here, a week there. She listened attentively, but I could see the problem eluded her. She sighed and said:

- Here I never feel that I am living. I feel that real life is out there, somewhere, waiting for me. What we have here in Poland, well, we live, but it is not a life...

I asked if she thought that life in Britain was more 'real' just because we had capitalism and unemployment. She thought for a long time before she replied. Clearly I was challenging some cherished dream.

- According to you, not.

- I think a lot of people in Britain would willingly swap Mrs Thatcher, the strong leader Poland so admires, for Lech Wałęsa, the charismatic trades union leader we need.

She shrugged, smiled her rich, wide, ironic smile and said:

- Maybe so.

I got up to make tea.

She flapped her hand at me, as if in jest.

- Why don't you sit and talk with me? You know I love it when we talk.

- OK. I have question. There are no political jokes anymore. Have you noticed? I mean the political joke was *the* Polish art form.

She shrugged:

- Everybody is too busy fighting the system. No-one has time to invent jokes when they are standing in a queue all day. Jokes take time. Somebody has to invent them and you do that sitting on a nice fat bottom in a nice warm office, sipping hot strong coffee with your friends. Now there's no coffee, no friends and the offices are cold. Everything is different now we have. Solidarność…. Oh, you! You are a thinking machine. You never stop. You're like a stomach, always growling at something, asking: What does this mean? Why is it like that? Why does somebody do this? Now you are frowning. You must learn to relax, to accept even that which you do not like.

*

I met Maria on the main square and we went for a short walk through town. Maria pointed with a gloved hand at a yellow painted building.

- You see that window? That's where Pope Jan Pawel stood. He sang songs to us from there.[43] It was the first time we felt ourselves, saw ourselves, as people, as a power. I felt, my God, there's millions of us. I felt then that we could do something. For the first time I had a positive feeling about my life. Communists, Catholics, we all had that. But I don't like the Pope. I don't trust him and his black-crow priests, and I don't trust Wałęsa either. They are all in bed together.

We stood looking at the window for a moment.

Later we went to Klub MPiK for coffee.[44] Often, when I was in town I would drop in to the Club to read the newspapers and magazines. It became a habit because sometimes they had coffee and condensed milk. The staff knew I was foreign and from my choice of newspapers guessed I was British. Anyway they had only to hear me speak to know that I was not Polish.

One day we went in and ordered coffee with condensed milk. The waitress looked at me, weighed my foreign-ness for a moment, looked Maria up and down, then said, very slowly:

- Excuse me sir, there was a big thunder storm in the night, you remember? And we keep all our tins of condensed milk stacked in the yard. Well the milk was struck by lightning and it all went sour. Would you like coffee without milk?

I thought it was very kind of her to explain. And yet, as a teacher that was a sentence that I would have thought

---

[43] Almost the first thing the Pope did on his election was to visit Poland in the spring of 1979.

[44] Klub Międzynarodowy Prasy i Książki - International Press and Book Club, a combination book shop, newspaper reading room and coffee shop with branches in most large towns.

extremely unlikely to occur, and therefore 'uncommunicative', too purely grammatical in form to be of any real use to a student. You live and you learn. I added the sentence 'My condensed milk has been struck by lightening' to my teaching repertoire.

We went up to the reading room and ordered coffee. When it came the staff explained there was no milk and no sugar, and it was powdered coffee, rather than grain. It was undrinkable. The faces all around the room seemed resigned to the collective discomfort. One man saw my distaste for the coffee and shrugged exaggeratedly as if to say: You're right, but that's how it is. Such times. We sat reading, slowly working our way through the whole intake: *Time*, *Newsweek*, *The Morning Star*, *The Guardian*, *The Times....* Sometimes the censor would cut out an article on Poland, just leaving a hole where the article had been. But censorship seemed to have collapsed. There was plenty about Poland, but nothing much that made any sense. We were interrupted by the arrival of a bearded journalist called Marek. I did not know him. He clearly had his eye on Maria and she was embarrassed to see him. I guessed they had once been a lot closer. He enquired why she had not been to see him for a while. He said he had some interesting new items in his collection and would like to show her. I asked what his collection consisted of, and from the look of horror on Maria's face I realised that I was not supposed to understand this conversation, let alone take part. Maria said in English:

- I don't think his collection would interest you.

Marek raised an eyebrow at her and reached into his pocket. He handed me a small package wrapped in tissue. Maria pushed back her chair in alarm. I unwrapped the package to find a slim bar of soap, no bigger than an after dinner mint. It had an eagle and letters embossed on it. Soap, white creamy soap. I sniffed it. Hardly scented at all. Maria said:

- Oh no, and gripping the arms of her chair she stared at the floor.

- You collect soap?

- No. Not just soap. Human soap. Made from Jews, I suppose. It cost me about 500 złoties, but I know how to get more. If you like I can give it to you...

Maria pushed back her chair and ran to the toilet. I also made a swift exit and threw up my sugarless, milkless, coffeeless coffee into the dirty toilet bowl. I washed the cold sweat from my face and mopped it dry with my handkerchief. At the toilet door Maria was waiting for me. She handed me my coat.

- I hope you don't mind. We are leaving.

Marek had taken our place in the reading room. He was drinking my coffee. On the way out Maria took a step towards Marek and said very quietly:

- Stay away from me, creep.

*

In September Maria and I decided to go north to the coast for a few days. We booked rooms in Gdańsk, at the Hotel Bałtyk. Maria was not sure about this. As she was from Kraków she did not regard the north and west, areas Poland had acquired in 1945, as 'real Poland', but she decided to give it a try anyway.[45]

---

[45]In 1945, as a result of the Yalta and Potsdam conferences, Poland lost vast expanses of territory in the east to the USSR. In exchange, Poland gained 116,000 square miles of territory in the west from defeated Germany, and set about expelling

Burning Worm

The holiday did not got off to a good start. We had agreed to meet at the station and catch the early morning train. She was waiting at a taxi-rank. It was about 4.30 in the morning. Suddenly a huge milicja paddy wagon pulled up next to her. Two milicja men jumped out and began to question her.

- Where are you going?
- To the railway station.
- Why?
- To meet my boy friend.
- What train are you getting?
- The one at ten minutes past five.
- I don't think so.
- Why not?
- I think you're going to miss your train.
- No, I'll get a taxi.
- There are no taxis.
- A girl like you should take care. You shouldn't be out alone at times like this.
- Pretty girl could come to some harm.
- I think you'd better come with us.
- But my train…
- Get in the back. Be a good girl and don't make a fuss.

One of the milicja-man took her by the elbow. She was terrified. She got in the truck and sat on a long bench. They locked the door and drove off at great speed. She had no idea what direction they were going in. After a few minutes the lorry stopped in a dark side street. She thought, this is it. They will rape me or beat me. One of

---

approximately 2.5 million Germans. This area comprised roughly 33% of postwar Polish territory. In effect the postwar Polish state had been moved 100 miles westwards.

the milicja-man opened the door and assisted her down. He said:

- The station is just around the corner. You would never have made it if you'd waited for a taxi. Sorry we couldn't take you right up to the front entrance, but your boyfriend would never forgive you if he saw you arrive in a milicja wagon.

They saw her confusion and laughed. She ran all the way to the station, and in the middle of the booking hall, she fell on me in floods of tears.

When we checked into the Hotel Bałtyk we could see Russian warships from our window, manoeuvring in the gulf.

Maria decided that however bare the shops might be, she wanted to go shopping and leave real exploring until later. I took this as a hint that she wanted a little breathing space and so I looked up my former students in the city and through them wangled an entry pass to the first Solidarność Congress which was then being held in the huge sports hall in Oliwa, just across the road from the office I had in my previous job, at the University of Gdańsk.

The Congress was both exciting and dull. The event itself was exciting, but in detail it was a meeting like any other. It had an agenda and motions for and against and speakers and disagreements and disputes and protestations. They were all there, the union big noises: Lech Wałęsa, Bogdan Lis, Anna Walentinowicz, Marian Jurczyk, Leszek Moczulski. There was a report that Soviet warships were landing Russian marines at night, but Wałęsa shrugged this off saying the work of the military - maneuvers and all - was nothing to do with the work of the trades union Solidarność, that people should stop worrying about things that did not concern them and get on with the business in hand.

There were subcommittees at work in meeting rooms and factions forming in corridors. Marian Jurczyk was arguing with someone about his anti-Semitic remarks in Szczecin earlier in the year. Jacek Kuroń was drawing out the intellectual renewal, persuading academics and historians to speak of their work in ways that were intelligible and useful to Polish working people. Adam Michnik argued:

- You cannot use the word socialism here: what Poland has is not socialism. The Party has appropriated the vocabulary and outward forms of socialism, yes, but without matching these things with the actual content of socialism.

Meanwhile on the main floor the general assembly of the union was debating whether or not to send fraternal greetings to the embryonic independent trades union movements of other East Bloc countries, thus encouraging the challenge not only to the central power of the Party and its leading role, but to the authority of the USSR itself. This was not something to be undertaken casually.

The Congress was enormously sober - in every sense of the word - and for all concerned was clearly hard, hard work. Most of the delegates had little sense of the processes of practical democracy. Everything - everything - had to be explained and worked out in painful detail. And, because Solidarność had grown tired of being misrepresented by the Party Press, it had banned Polish journalists from the Congress. I'd had enough of the intense atmosphere. I was deadly tired of the struggle. Watching these frail, weary, decent people try to repair and restore honesty and responsibility to their individual and collective life was exhausting.

I took the tram along Wita Stwosza and met up with Maria. We took a walk through the drizzle to the Neptune fountain. Neptune was busy threatening the tourists with his trident, as usual. Just next to the fountain there was a hole in the ground and some students were digging and sifting the mud. A man in a dirty white coat supervised. It was an archaeological dig. Maria asked if they had found anything interesting. The man in the white coat, who it seems was a professor, said they had found a charred area and some fish bones.

- Here, in this very spot, several thousand years ago, maybe five or six thousand, a proto-Pole sat down to a breakfast of flounder.

I asked how he knew it was a proto-Pole. Could it have been a Celt or a wandering Scandinavian, a German, a Balt? The man looked at me suspiciously and said, no he was certain it was a proto-Pole. I asked how he could tell: did the Poles build their fires differently from other people? How could he be sure? The Professor just said:

- Trust me. I know these things. I am sure.

- Yes, but how do you know?

The students stopped digging. The Professor said:

- Young man, I don't think you have a full grasp of the situation. He poked me in the chest with his finger. It is a proto-Pole.

Maria dragged me away saying:

- Don't make trouble. Walk away. I have to live in this fucking country, remember.

We went for a drink in the Amber Bar on Targ Węglowy. It was a place I liked, but as soon as we walked in I knew something was not quite right. The waitress shuffled over and stood at our table glowering at two men in the far corner - the only other customers. She pushed a lock of hair behind her ear, wiped the table and said under her breath:

- Shipyard workers!

We ordered two lemon teas.

- No lemons, said the waitress.

- Two lemon teas without lemon, I said. She smiled. In the corner one of the men was flourishing a huge wad of paper money in her direction. She wrote our order on her note pad and went off to see what the men wanted.

I watched fascinated. They were so drunk they could barely keep their eyes open. They blinked like owls. How they had got like this was something of a mystery because in Gdańsk - as in most of Poland throughout the Solidarność period - it was as dry as America during Prohibition. Now the two shipyard workers wanted cognac. As if by magic the waitress brought them two glasses of cognac. She said:

- This is the last. Drink up and then out you go.

They rumbled complaint but agreed.

Over tea I asked Maria about her marriage - it was the only time we talked about it.

She did not seem to resent the divorce - only lamented her innocence in getting married in the first place. Or rather, in getting married to this particular man.

Her husband drank a lot. She knew this before she married him. It was not remarkable. Among young Poles drinking is de rigeur, a demonstration of masculinity, of heroism, of Polishness, of that spirit of being agin' whatever there is to be agin'. Maria knew her husband drank a lot, but she married him anyway. In the months

190

after the wedding his drinking hit unbelievable levels. She said he drank constantly:

- I mean he would drink at the breakfast table, at lunch time, at tea time. It got so that although you could smell the vodka on his breath, you could not tell he had been drinking from his behaviour. He behaved absolutely normally.

They had been married for about four months when they began to wonder why it was that although they had not been using contraception, Maria was not yet pregnant. They tried to discuss the subject, but discussion immediately degenerated into a row, with each other's shortcomings on parade. He ended up getting stinking drunk, and she in order to placate, him agreed that probably there was something wrong with her and that she would see a doctor. Next day, as part of the making-up process - he was mighty hung over and feeling guilty about the things they had said - she managed to persuade him that he ought to see the doctor too - just in case. She said:

- I don't know why I did that. I was sure the fault was mine. My Catholic guilt. We had done it before we were married. I was punished for being a harlot. Anyway, isn't it always the woman who is to blame? Her equipment is so much more complicated.

They went jointly to their family doctor and he sent them to see specialists. Maria suffered a whole range of pushing, palpating, poking and painful indignities before the doctors - all male - wrote her a report that said on account of a rare hormone imbalance she was extremely unlikely to ever have children. Perhaps if they could find a pill that would regulate her wayward hormones then her body might - just might - be induced towards regularity, and she might just get pregnant. But it would all have to be very carefully timed. It would demand great patience and persistence from her husband. She showed me the paper the doctors had given her, much crumpled, begrimed and tear stained. She carried it in her handbag. The international recipe, the doctor's inexplicable illiterate scrawl, was undoubtedly authentic.

That night she showed the paper to her husband. She expected they would sit and hold hands, that he would comfort her.

- They had told me that I was not a real woman. I wanted Staszek to put his arms around me.

She thought vaguely they might adopt a child. It was a foolish hope. Staszek listened in silence to what she said. He grew very angry, saying that she had lied to him about being healthy, that he had been duped into marrying her. She protested that the doctors had said she could have a baby under certain circumstances.... but he did not want to hear it. He went out with his buddies and did not come back that night.

I could imagine how his friends teased him. Four months and no bun in the oven, Staszek. Are you sure you're doing it right, Staszek? The doctor can show you a rubber model, or there's a picture on the toilet wall, Staszek...

- He never talked about having children before we got married. I don't think he thought about them very much. But, you know, after we got married, after he had 'taken a girl and turned her into a woman', as the phrase goes, the next thing, the next demonstration of his manhood was to get me pregnant. No?

Hardly had they recovered from this blow when the results of Staszek's tests arrived. The doctor from the hospital had appended a note saying that in his view, and he had given Staszek a thorough check up, his poor motility was the result of excessive alcohol consumption. If he were to give up the booze now and forever, this position, though it could never be entirely reversed, might be improved upon. He also recommended that Staszek should give up wearing long underwear in favour of cotton shorts, even in winter, and that he should abstain from intercourse for most of the month, saving his seed for when his wife told him she was ovulating. The hospital took the trouble to send an expensive imported Swedish thermometer specially for this purpose.

Staszek was speechless with rage. He opened a bottle of vodka and started boozing without even bothering to find a glass. After two hours of solid drinking he had not spoken a word. Finally he got up and went out on a week long spree. Once he was brought home by his buddies. Once he was found asleep on the stairs outside the apartment. And once a kindly militiaman brought him home, saying he knew where the boy lived and did not want to see him in trouble.

Like most young couples Maria and Staszek shared a tiny apartment with her parents and her grandmother. Her parents were reluctant to intervene in the daughter's marriage, but offered whatever support they could.

One evening Staszek started drinking again.

- It was after eleven in the evening. I was in bed and he was opening a second half litre of vodka.

Maria said something to him. Staszek replied by taking the expensive thermometer from the bedside table - she had in fact been trying to set in motion the solution the doctors suggested - and he snapped it in two. Maria realised that to buy a new thermometer would be impossible. The meaning of his action was not wasted on her. She leapt out of bed. Maybe she gave him a push. She says she did not. But what else can you do or say in that situation?

Staszek hit her very hard and called her *kórwa*.[46] Maria ran naked from her bed, into her parents' room. There her father, who had guessed what was taking place in the next room was already up and dressed in string vest and trousers.

I thought Maria was about to say her father strode into the marriage chamber and strengthened by righteous anger, wiped out the drunken sot with one blow of his mighty paw. Staszek may have been frightening for Maria, but he held no terror for her father - a man of remarkable patience and tolerance. Without laying a hand on Staszek, Maria's father propelled the drunk out of the flat simply by bouncing him with his large round tummy. Telling me about it Maria laughed until tears of shame and joy ran down her cheeks.

- And then, she said, we threw his clothes out into the hallway after him. And daddy said to him: You, you are banned from this place.

That night Maria sat up late with her parents. She decided she did not want Staszek back. She phoned Staszek's parents and next morning they came round to pick up his clothes. She spoke with Staszek only once after that, to agree the division of the little property they owned jointly: thus Maria was left with a superb West German tape deck but no speakers. And Staszek was left with superb West German speakers, but no tape deck. It made no sense, but that was how it had to be. Apart from

---

[46]Possibly derived from Latin meaning curve or slit. Polish slang: cunt.

the formal court hearing to annul the marriage she never saw Staszek again.

- I'm glad it was a civil wedding. If it had been a Church job I'd never have got out.

- Was it an easy decision to make? I asked. I mean you seem to have decided very quickly that you did not want him back.

- Ah but you must remember that I cannot tell you everything of this story. You see he was my first lover. But by this time I thought if this is sex, then it is not worth all the fuss and certainly not worth this kind of trouble. Later I had other lovers and realised that my husband was just a brute - indifferent, clumsy. Now I know what to look for in a man. I don't make the same mistake any more.

She looked away quickly, clapping her hand across her mouth as if something awful was about to fly out. But above the hand her eyes still smiled.

In the corner one of the two drinkers stood up uncertainly. He swayed a moment and flourished his wad of notes at the waitress. Reluctantly she went over to them. The man's voice boomed:

- Now we have Solidarność I'm a rich man. You're a pretty girl, why don't you marry me, eh?

The other shipyard worker tugged at his sleeve and crooned.

- Jasio, Jasio. Behave.

- Quite right. Better not. Got a wife. Don't want two, eh? But rich. Eh? Look at it. Anh? All this.... money. And what can I do with it? I'll tell you what I can do with it. Nothing. Can't even buy toilet paper. Can't do shit. So maybe I'd better save the money to wipe my...

- Right, you two. Out. The waitress pushed a chair aside. I'm not having language like that in here.

The man blinked at her.

- I wanted to buy a kitchen table. A kitchen table, you know? He indicated its size and shape with waving hands. But I can't find a kitchen table to buy. There's no tables. No chairs. No cupboards. I've got the money. I earned it, see? But nothing to spend it on. It's just paper...

The man threw his money on the table in a greasy pile and collapsed in his chair, his head on top of the money. His friend leaned over and rubbed his neck:

- Jasio, Jasio. Don't take on so. It'll work out. You'll see.

He rose to his feet and turned to the waitress.

- Please miss. Don't judge my friend too harshly. He's not a worm. He's a good man. But you know how it is. He doesn't mean to offend. His wife threatened to leave him. The table was supposed to be a.... a.... He waved his hand, but could not find the words. To make good, you know. Anyway.... we don't mean to offend.

He bent in a low bow and kissed the waitress's hand. She allowed it, but was not impressed.

- It's the same for everybody, she said.

- You are right. But worse on some days than on others, don't you agree? Now, be a good girl and give us a bottle and we'll be on our way. Right? Here's a.... what is that? 10,000 złoty? Anyway, keep the change. He handed her a note from the pile. The note was worth about five times the value of the cognac.

The waitress brought a bottle and helped the men negotiate the doorway into the street. Maria sat rigid, and only relaxed when they were safely outside.

The waitress brought two glasses of cognac to our table.

- On the house, she said. By way of apology.

- How do you manage to sell cognac? Officially, it's prohibition. No?

She smiled and said:

- Officially? This is mine. It doesn't belong to the cafe. When I saw how things were shaping up I laid in a store of the stuff - spent all my savings. Smartest thing I ever did. Word soon gets around. I'm making about a thousand percent profit on every glass.

We drank to her health and then she went to clear up the other tables. Maria said:

- This girl has good business sense. But now perhaps you see why I worry? You tell me these are honest people. But look at them. This girl, the waitress, she knows what they are, she knows how to treat them. Monsters, pickled like cucumbers. Can you see that?

- No, I lied. I can't see that.

We finished our cognac in silence.

class war

A class spy is a worrying thing to have. The first time I became aware of it was when, in accordance with the regulations I set a summer exam. On the day of the exam I noted that several of my students were absent. I did not think much about it at the time. Then about a week later I found a note on my desk from one of the absent students. The note was in Polish. It said: 'Please don't forget to enter my exam result in the *Protokoly*. I had a result of 70%.'[47] When I deciphered the signature I was amazed to see that the note was from one of the poorest students in

---

[47]Protokoły: student records.

the class. Such a high mark was most improbable - hence the note was in Polish.

I went to the *Protokoly* and looked up his entry only to find that someone else had examined him and had indeed awarded a mark of 70%. That someone was the head of the department. When I checked, all the absentees were there, all with improbably high marks and all examined by the head of the department.

It took me a little time to work out what was going on, but it seems the milicja used the *Protokoly* to find students who were in danger of failing. They would then offer a guaranteed pass in return for information. Once the milicja had the student the only way out was either to pass duff information to the milicja and hope they never realised, or to improve so dramatically that they escaped the danger of failing altogether. This last option does not seem to have been much exercised.

I asked Maria about this and she said:

- Don't worry about the class spy. Sure he's there, but if you think about it, it is not a system that should ever worry a language teacher. You see, if your student is so bad he needs the milicja to help him, then they are probably too poor in English to inform accurately anyway.

Once, when I was teaching in Gdańsk, we had a class spy. Bogdan turned up to the first class of the new year. He had failed his exams and the re-sits three times in three years. I was more than surprised to see him.

- Good morning Bogdan. I did not expect to see you here.

- Prosze?[48]

Bogdan was polite, but English was not his strong point, even after three years of university English. Not to

---

[48] *Prosze* - Please.

put too fine a point on it, Bogdan was a dunce and after reading through his examination script I had no hesitation whatsoever in recommending that his studies be terminated. Yet here he was, about to enter the new academic year without having passed a single one of his exams. I was so angry I was raving in the staff room. Ela, the departmental secretary, waving newly crimsoned, still wet fingernails at me said, said:

- Ah, you don't know about Bogdan. His father was at school with Tadeusz Fiszbach, the Gdańsk Party chief. He's nothing but a simple worker, but he uses his connections well. Bogdan got extra points at his entrance exam for being the son of a worker. His father did the rest. Bogdan always fails his exams, even his entrance exams. He's been expelled twice. He shouldn't even be here. But his father comes and speaks to the Rector, and Bogdan comes slouching in again with that stupid grin of his. If I were you I would ignore it altogether. Don't expect any work from him. Oh, one more thing. Don't tell jokes in his presence, jokes about Poland or politics or the milicja. One of the other students told me that his father can get him back in here because his son is a milicja informer. Nothing definite, you know, but there is no smoke without fire, and in his case I cannot see how it could be otherwise...

I did try to get work out of Bogdan, but Ela was right, it was hopeless. He did not do a stroke of work. He was not interested in anything. He should not have been at university in the first place, and certainly not after repeatedly failing his exams. His vocabulary was limited to a list of football clubs and some fairly startling remarks [half in Polish, half in English] about the virtues and physical characteristics of the girls in his class. I gave up.

But what did he tell the milicja? He cannot have told them much. His English was not good enough to even follow what was going on in the classroom, so if his target was me, then the exercise was a waste of time. At one routine interview with the milicja they demonstrated that they were remarkably well informed about my love life, but totally ignorant about everything that happened at the university. After a series of long silences the milicja officer said:

- Your department is crazy. All of them. So many pretty girls, so many stupid boys, so many neurotic teachers. I don't suppose any of them are even screwing each other, are they? What about the teachers, are they screwing? With each other? With the students?

Bogdan cannot have had anything to tell these people. Maybe he wasn't a spy after all. Or maybe he was a spy, but a very bad one. Perhaps Military Intelligence is, after all, a contradiction in terms.

*

As part of the run-up to examinations, I decide to revise the conditionals in class. At the end of the lesson I ask the students to produce a conditional sentence of their own. After a couple of minutes Grzegorz, well known as a local Party man, and sporting a huge Friends of the Soviet Union badge, stood up:

- When you are in USA [as usual he misses out the definite article and pronounces it OoEssAh] then if you got free.

I did not know which was more incredible, the grammatical mish-mash or the fact that a Party member can say this. My face must have run a gamut of emotions as I struggled to find an appropriate reaction. In the end I just stood there with my mouth open. The class too roared with laughter, delighted at my dilemma. Grzegorz too seemed mighty pleased with himself.

If I had my way I would ban the words 'free' and freedom unless used in a specific context. Free from. Freedom to. Otherwise these words just encourage hopeless fantasies. I wanted to scream at Grzegorz: 'Freedom from what you idiot? Freedom to starve in your own time? Freedom to be unemployed? Freedom to do just what, exactly?' But I can't. It is a cultural and political problem, but also it is a human problem of perception, experience, understanding. I can't say this because here people are already starving. Here people get their unemployment benefit on the job. Yes his life would be materially better in the USA. This problem is so huge I cannot begin to grapple with it. It is not the kind of problem you can reduce to a language exercise in class. I am too tired. I feel I have run into a brick wall so I stick to the textbook and the rest of the lesson is without interest. The students sense my unhappiness, but they are aware that their dreams are at stake. If they ask, I might just tell them what I think. But if I damage their dreams, where would we be?

In Conrad's *Heart of Darkness* Marlow has his rivets to play with at moments of crisis. At the end of the class I murmur:

- Rivets.

The class look at me blankly.

Burning Worm

*

Talking with one of my postgraduate students in the break I realise that he is a milicja-man I ask him why he wants to learn English. He looks at me with a raised eyebrow and says:
- Well, there is more money in keeping an eye on foreigners like you than in ordinary duties.

He says this casually, and then goes on to say that the prisons have all been emptied: 23,000 petty criminals have been amnestied and sent home to make way for politicos when the army stages its coup. I have heard this from other sources too, but anyway I tell him he's crazy. The Polish army would never do such a thing. The army is loyal to Poland. And as soon as I say this, as soon as the words leave my lips, I ask myself what I can possibly mean. Loyal to Poland? Loyal to whose Poland? Maybe I'm going loopy. If the army is told to walk through flaming hoops, it will do it, and it will do it for Poland. In fact the head-banging professional soldiers would probably enjoy walking through flaming hoops. This is something I have not thought about sufficiently. The milicja-man sees what is going on behind my eyes. He smiles and nods. Product of the west that I am, the thought of the coup gives me problems that the threat of a Russian invasion does not.
- I know what you are thinking, he says. You are wondering how any self respecting intelligent Pole can have anything to do with the authorities. Though, of course, the question is better left unsaid. But I think that only through saying and revealing the unpleasant, suppressed side of this society will it become sane, will it be able to come face to face with itself. How long can this

confrontation be delayed? Only as long as the Party is in control. As soon as the Party loses its grip, Poland and Poles will have to become responsible for themselves - for their past and for their future - whether they like it or not. And that is why Solidarność cannot succeed. Poles do not want to be responsible. Perhaps I am in the wrong, but I doubt that I will ever be punished for what I do. Not that what I do is so very awful, and anyway, I'm sure that the security services in the west keep an eye on all foreigners too, so...

He shrugs.

Later I spoke with another of our mature students. I knew he had graduated in Polish studies from Kraków University and had written his masters thesis on Polish anthropology - a study of folk art in the Tatra mountains - before joining the milicja and rising to the rank of major. We sat in a cafe while he explained his view of the situation to me.

- The West has got Poland all wrong. That's nothing new of course. You see Polish life - the history, culture, institutions - its whole existence lies in plotting, cheating and conniving. If you look at our history, at the years before the Partitions you will see what I mean. Thousands of lords all making deals, falling out, back-stabbing. And if you look at the Partition you'll see that it was a perfect breeding ground for plots and factions, secret societies, pointless revolutions, code words - all that juvenile paraphernalia. They loved all that, and they still do. Look at Poland now. Where are the poets and artists and writers? Censorship has almost ceased to exist, but are the writers saying anything? You can kiss my arse if they are. They have nothing to say. They looked as if they might have something to say when there was censorship, but now, when we need their intelligence, their independence and their moral senses, they are silent. They are only important as long as they are suppressed. They are a kind of folk hero, but they are out of business for the moment. Oh don't worry, everything will be back to normal when the military make their move and everybody feels suppressed again. Then we will all know what is what again. The fact is that codes and plots and secrets, that is the real Poland. Without the milicja, the priests, the poets would be nothing; without the milicja and the authorities, without strong leadership, repression if you like to call it that, there is no Poland. Without the milicja the Catholic church would have collapsed years ago. How long do you think the Polish priesthood - a bunch of rural mental midgets - would survive in a free and open society?

girl & grandfather

My balcony in Kraków overlooked a children's playground and a kindergarten. At three o clock every day, an old man would appear at the playground. He was accompanied by a girl in a red anorak. She was aged about twelve or thirteen. She wore the anorak no matter what the weather. I had the impression that her health was delicate. I don't think she was his daughter, but I may be wrong. I think she was his granddaughter. From the way she walked it was clear that she was brain damaged in some way. When he stopped, she also stopped. She would stand with her toes turned in, her fingers in her mouth, swaying from side to side. Her eyes flickered from one object to the next with no obvious curiosity.

If there were children present on the playground, the Grandfather would stroll over to them and offer them a few złoties or some biscuits. His gestures made it clear that he was hiring the kids to play with her. The kids usually took the money, but the game was always short. After a few minutes one of them would remember an errand they had to run, and then one by one the others would slide off too, leaving the girl in the anorak standing with her fingers in her mouth. She was several inches taller than any of the kids who used the playground, so I suppose she was a couple of years older too.

When the kids had gone, Grandfather would take a large brightly coloured plastic ball from his bag, and positioning himself a few feet from the girl he would throw the ball for her to catch. Her coordination was poor. Sometimes she didn't see the ball at all, other times she would lunge at it, her arms flailing. But the result was always the same: the ball went bouncing past her and Grandfather would have to go and retrieve it. After several minutes of this Grandfather would lose his temper and shout at her, at which she would begin to cry. When she cried, Grandfather became ashamed of himself and throwing the ball away from him, he would run up to her and hug her. They would stay locked like this in the middle of the playground for several minutes together. Then he would take out his handkerchief and wipe her face. When he had finished, he would wipe his own face because he cried too. In a whole year I only ever saw her catch the ball once.

They always finished with an attempt at the slide. This was a steel frame with a set of steps and a chute that stood in the middle of the playground. At first, she would not take more than a step up the ladder before beginning to wail. Then it was two steps. And slowly her confidence grew. Over a period of several months she actually made it to the top of the slide frame, and eventually she sat there. But that was the limit of her ambition. Nothing Grandfather could do would persuade her to let go and launch herself down the slide. Other kids pushed past her and whizzed down. Her Grandfather actually paid kids to show her how it was done. But she refused to slide. After a while Grandfather brought a box with him, and stood it at the side of the slide so that he could hold onto her anorak from the back. But she, gripping the sides of the slope with knuckles gleaming white with pressure even against the white of the freshest winter snow, would only let herself down inch by inch. There was no joy to be had in this though and Grandfather wanted her to let go, to do it for herself, to whizz where other kids whizzed. Whenever she thought he was about to let go she would scream with fear and turn on her stomach, blocking the chute completely until she felt again his grip on her anorak and she inched herself down.

The day she slid right to the bottom of the chute with no knuckle grip and no anorak safety-hold was really quite something. I was on the balcony at the time. Watching while the three o clock pantomime went on as usual. She failed to hold the attention of the kids, failed to catch the ball, and sat sullenly at the top of the slide. No progress today, I told myself. But she had positioned herself a little further forward than she realised, and when she let go the side to adjust her hat she suddenly found herself whizzing earthwards. She landed flat on her back at the bottom of the chute before she had time to scream. For a moment she looked as if she was about to start crying. Her mouth opened in a huge grimace, but the cry changed from one of fear to one of delight. She grinned from ear to ear, and I swear that I could have counted every tooth in her head, if I had been so inclined. She threw her face up to the sky and hugged herself chuckling and chuckling. Grandfather, concerned for her safety, ran from his box to the front of the slide. And I who could see from my balcony vantage point that she was more than perfectly safe, but also perfectly happy with herself, I completely lost control and yelled out for all I was worth:

- Yeah! Hurray! Hurray!

Grandfather heard my noise. If the sight of a grown man leaping around cheering and clapping surprised him he did not show it. He took off his cap, bowed deeply and then waved to me. The girl was already on her feet and racing past him round to the steps for another try. The old man watched her, shrugged at me with his arms wide as if to say: Kids... and then he hurried after her. Next day I noticed him look up to my balcony. I stepped out and waved. He waved. He pointed me out to the girl and she too waved. I begin to feel I belong. I have neighbours.

flight

Maria and I sat up late talking, talking, talking. The two of us in a pool of lamplight, the rest of the apartment in darkness. In the distance a dog barked and from the railway yards came the vague clanking of a Warsaw bound goods train. Maria had been reading an article I had written. She sighed as she put it aside.

- You are right and you are wrong. I think it would be better if you didn't write that it takes so many years to save up for a car in Poland, or how difficult it is to get a flat. It gives westerners a bad impression. Yes, we know these things are true, but if you say these things then you are measuring this system against the west and using the west's measuring stick. A westerner reading this will accept it as a straight comparison. They'll say: 'Shit, I'm better off here.' Tell me honestly, do you miss TV in Poland? Do you ever lack entertainment. You are richer in spirit without your TV and your consumer culture. You make your own entertainment Poland is just outside the normal run of things, and you have to make allowances for that difference. If you look at the purely material aspects you miss the good points altogether, you miss the people themselves. We know the place is a mess, the system is shit. But do me a favour and don't help Thatcher and Reagan with this sort of comparison. You only encourage them.

Later that evening Maria said:

- What do you mean when you say in your article that we should not want what you have in the west?

- Well it's difficult to explain, but basically I think the west for most Poles is just this wondrous place full of goodies. They see all the wealth and the luxury, the success. But they don't see the work it took to create that wealth, and they don't see the pain and the waste and the poverty. I think if you knew the west better you would not want it quite so hard.

- But if you live here in Poland you must look somewhere for a real life...

- I'm not saying don't look.

- You think we should stay communist and live in this mess?

- East and west are both a mess, but they are different kinds of mess. All I'm saying is that maybe Poles will have the opportunity to build something else - not east or west, not capitalist, not communist...

- Why haven't you asked me to go to Britain with you?
- Because I am afraid you will say no.
- Perhaps I will say yes. Ask me.
- OK. Maria, will you come to Britain with me?
- No.

She put her hand over mine and said wearily:

- I listen to Voice of America. I listen to Radio Free Europe. I know what is what in the world. What would I do in the west? I am an expert in preserving baroque and renaissance Polish architecture. There is not so much scope for that outside Poland. I am Polish. Adapted to Polish conditions. To live anywhere else would make a nonsense of me.

And that was that.

*

From where I stand in the angle of the main Market Square I can see a crowd waiting to buy cinema tickets, a crowd waiting for the international [which, of course, means Soviet] book shop to open, a crowd waiting to enter the almost empty delicatessen, a queue waiting for the chemist to open, and a queue to enter the restaurant. Behind me, I don't even have to look, to know that it is there, a queue of several hundred waits at the butcher's shop, and over the street a line trails three or four wide to the government alcohol store where it is rumoured there is beer. The travel agent is full to bursting so the door cannot be opened. The queue at the bread shop mingles with that of the butcher. It is what the Poles would call a train crash.[49] When the rumour spreads that the bread shop has cakes or sugar, people leave the one queue for the other. I have ration cards for meat, flour, sugar, rice, butter, fat, oil and buckwheat. But these things are not in the shops for me to use the cards. I have a huge pile of ration tickets but no food. Definition of a Polish sandwich: a meat coupon between two bread coupons. Joke! I am over 18 years, so I cannot buy chocolate, even if I could find any to buy. At my local baker they start queuing at 07.00: the shop does not open until 10.00. Politicians cannot read the writing on the wall: union officials believe their own propaganda. This can only end in tears.

*

My last day in Poland. Maria and I are both in a foul temper. Maria does her best to be pleasant. She is angry I am leaving. She understands things have not gone well for me here, that this place was killing me with tension and shortages. She thinks my fears of a coup are just paranoia, even though she had mentioned it to me in the first place. She thinks I should just reverse the decision and stay. For her it is that simple. I have tried to explain that I would not survive.

I take a last walk, a last look, around the Azory housing estate. It is evening, already dark and misty. The place is about to howl with boredom. You can feel the boredom in the air, smell it even. It is time for the main evening news on TV. As I walk around the estate's main square I notice that the evening is illuminated by the steady blue-grey flicker of TV. On almost every balcony there is a TV set,

---

[49]A pun. In Polish the word for a small train and for a queue are the same.

switched on, with the sound turned down. Nothing moves on the street. There was not a human being in sight. But on balcony after balcony the same head and shoulders silently mouth in the gloom. When I reach the end of my block somebody has spray painted the wall with the wavy wriggling outlines of a worm, and along its back is the message: 'TV kłamie'.[50]

*

I wait for customs to check my luggage. Maria stands quietly and I can see she is doing her damnedest not to cry, but that just makes it worse.

- You will return? When? To visit, to talk?
- As soon as I can. A couple of months. In the New Year. I have promised.

I lean over the barrier to kiss her. She murmurs:

- So you are going then...
- But I will be back soon.

In the departure lounge I sit staring at the wall in rigid concentration.

On the tarmac two soldiers, teenagers in camouflage, festooned with grenades and weighed down by huge carbines, played 'Stone, Scissors, Paper' behind the fuel tender. Next to me on the plane a woman blesses herself and prays to the Blessed Virgin Mary.

The plane taxies, turns and then lurches into the sky. The patchwork blanket of Poland falls away and fades beneath a leaden fume. Above there is bright, painful sunlight. The sun beams indifferent on east and west alike. Over the Baltic a West German fighter plane closes and settles at our port wing. It stays with us past Denmark, its

---

[50]TV kłamie - TV Lies.

silver glinting against the gunmetal grey of the North Sea, then it dives away toward Holland leaving nothing but an oily feather to mark its track.

The woman next to me returns from the toilet, commences prayers to another saint in her pantheon, pausing only to tell me that she has stolen the toilet roll but if I want to go I have only to ask and she will slide me a wad.

- It's West German, she says. Very Soft.

The stewardess comes around with coffee and notices my distress.

- If the sun is too strong, she says, you can slide down the blind.

When she returns to offer a second cup she slides a small packet of handkerchiefs into my lap. She has been to Poland before. She knows it is not the sun that forces the tears.

final

I had information, intuition, the evidence of my own eyes, that Poland had come closer to open military confrontation with the USSR than most people in the west realised, and that if this were to be staved off for much longer the Polish military or the Party or the milicja - somebody, anybody with a shred of power and authority left - would have to make a move to crush Solidarność. Before the Soviets lost patience.

But the chaos went further than that. The prisons had been emptied of 23,000 prisoners, as a result there was a massive crime wave. There were epidemics of hepatitis and tuberculosis. There were hunger marches. Maria's father had slipped me a Party document carefully marked as *For Internal Party Use Only* which showed not only that the crime rate was up by 26%, but also gave a detailed statistical breakdown showing the devastating impact of the past year on the economy. It showed secret production figures, estimates for the future. Maria's father said: 'Show this to people in the west. Let them know what is really happening here. I'm sure your journalists only see what the Party wants them to report.... you watch, I'm also sure this will be dismissed as black propaganda'.

*

I half expected to be stopped by Special Branch at the airport. But no. They let me through without a word. In London I telephoned *The Times*, *The Guardian*, *The Financial Times*, *The New Statesman*, *The Economist*. I never got beyond the sub-editor and the response was always the same:

- No we haven't heard anything at all about a military coup. Rumours, yes, but if there was something beyond that, I think we'd know, don't you? You can't keep a thing like that secret for long.... What you are offering us is nothing more than gossip. You have a document? Well, perhaps it was foolish to smuggle it out.... Yes, but documents of that nature.... Even so, I doubt we could trust what you have.... I mean, ask yourself, why was a member of the Party giving you such a document? Look, we have our own journalists to take care of all that for us.... Frankly, the reading public is sick of Solidarność. And Poland. They've had it nearly every day for a year.... Yes, of course you can leave your name and address.

Burning Worm

*

On 14 December 1981, the day after the military declared Martial Law, the day after Poland invaded itself, I sat in front of the TV watching the snippets of newsreel that had somehow managed to escape the military net, trying to imagine what was happening, puzzling out what it all meant. I tried repeatedly to ring Maria in Kraków but the operator said the lines were cut. So I waited for the phone to ring. I waited for the newspaper editors I had tried to alert over the previous two weeks to contact me, to ask questions. I waited for someone, somewhere to take an interest. I waited for someone to want to make sense of this terrible mess. Nobody rang.

*

After several failed efforts, I finally managed to get a visa and returned to Poland. The country was still under Martial Law. Travelling from Warsaw to Kraków by train, opposite me sat an army colonel. Without hesitation as soon as he realised I was foreign he started to talk keenly. He took me to task for the simplistic attitudes the western leaders and press were displaying towards the government of General Jaruzelski.

- It's all very well to say that the army has betrayed Poland. In the short term it may appear that way. But the alternative was that the Russians would have done the job for us. Reluctantly perhaps, but they would have done it. And don't tell me of the violence. Fewer people died in imposing Martial Law than die in an average day of violence by the Reagan financed death squads of south America. There is simply no comparison. In years to come Europe will thank us - east and west. Poland was on the brink of total disintegration: we could not physically have survived another winter of chaos. General Jaruzelski said this at the time, but then it was not convenient to believe him. The fact is that professional soldiers, officers like myself, sympathise with many of the aims of Solidarność. We want the things they want. And we all know that there is a lot wrong with this place. But Solidarność was riddled with trouble makers and opportunists - in fact, just like the Party. And don't forget, we banned both Solidarność and the Party. They were about as bad as each other, worms burrowing into the body of the nation. We had to clean out the whole lot and start again on our terms. With the army its different. We don't negotiate. We take advice, decide what needs to be done, and then give orders. If we say reform this department in such a way, then it is reformed. If it is not reformed, then we want to know why. And the army is saying reform. If only people would listen to us they would find that the army is the only thing that feeds them and protects them, that stands between them and the Russians, between them and themselves...

Looking around the compartment I realised that everyone was listening to our conversation. But as the Colonel took a long drag on his cigarette and leaned back in his seat, the other passengers, as one, looked out of the windows with a fixed and glassy stare.

*

In a Kraków coffee bar where there was only tea, I got into conversation with two men. They were keen to tell a Westerner of their experiences under the military government. The shorter of the two said:

- I was in a cafe when the riot police arrived. They threw in tear gas and when we came out they beat us to the pavement with truncheons. My friend here was in the Lenin Shipyards in Gdańsk when the tanks pushed in the gates. He tried to jam a crowbar in the caterpillar tracks, but it didn't work.

As if to illustrate just why it did not work, the taller of the two men took his arm from his coat pocket and showed a wrist stump where a hand should have been. He placed the wrist carefully on the table top and slowly unwound a pair of women's tights to reveal the scar and the stitching. His friend said:

- He lost two toes and a hand trying to stop that tank. He keeps the tights on the wrist to protect it from the cold. He can't keep a glove on, you see. Isn't that right?

The taller man did not answer. He was winding the tights back around his wrist. His breath rasped as he did so. A cigarette dangled from his lip. I watched as a single bead of sweat detached itself from his hairline and ran down the side of his face.

*

When I met Maria again she pulled away from me saying.

- No. We have had a war here. It can't be like it was between us.

That was practically the only exchange we managed. The rest, as they say, was silence.

*

Nothing is certain. Maybe nothing ever was. But now everything is much less certain than before. Joseph

Burning Worm

Conrad said: 'before the Congo I was just an animal'. A worm maybe. I feel the same about Poland. Things are different now... My walk has changed. My shoulders are rounded now. My head, thrust forward, jars with each step. My feet hit the floor hard, bite even into concrete. My heels are sore, as if some head wound has upset my sense of balance. Once I could wear a pair of shoes for a year before they needed repair. Now after a few months they are beyond repair.

*

In the end we are made perfect. We are, after all, over thirty years of age. And our town, our friendly enemy, conducts long serious conversations with us still. After all, it seems, the world has not quite given up on us. But at night voices set us off, a distant whistle orders us out to struggle, to travel to distant places, towns we know only from our dreams. The dawn finds us unprepared for our departure: the bone comb as yet unpacked. But still we are not homeless, exactly. We have our dreams. We are housed in dreams. In the end we are made perfect.

postscript

I believed I had finished my editorial work, but was no nearer to solving the riddles surrounding the enigmatic Eugene Hinks, when a letter arrived from 'Maria'. With her permission I reprint the letter here in the belief it sheds useful light on *Burning Worm*.

Respected Sir,
You must excuse me for not wishing to see you or talk about my relationship with Eugene. For me it is a painful memory. I had no wish to be reminded of him. Especially when I hoped I had finally found happiness. But that is another story.

Upon reflection I have to say I can tell you very little about Eugene. Although the long months of Martial Law prevented us from meeting, I think you should know that Eugene sent me and my family food parcels from England. How he arranged this I never could find out, but in this way he helped keep us going through very dark times.

I have read both Kochanowski's and Żółty's books on the subject, but what they do not say is that Eugene did in fact manage to get back into Poland, just before Martial Law was lifted in July 1983. He could be very determined - did you know that about him?

During this visit we agreed to marry, and that I would move to England. Everything here was such a mess then, and there was no possibility of him coming to live in Poland. He had enough of the place. Understandable. He returned to England saying he would arrange some sort of course for me to convert my qualifications so they would be acceptable in British universities. I had given him photocopies of all my certificates and documents. But after this I had only a couple of letters from him, then nothing.

After a while I gave up waiting, became involved with someone else. The next time Eugene showed up in Poland I would not meet him. My father met him though, and criticised him for not writing to me. But later my father told me Eugene was quite bewildered by this, saying he had written frequently, but had no reply from me. A mystery.

Then, in 1992 some months after the collapse of communism, a small package arrived at my flat. The package consisted of the missing letters Eugene had written to me. They were in a plastic bag supplied by the Polish Post Office. On the outside of the bag was written 'Damaged in Transit'. But in fact none of the letters had been damaged. They had not even been opened, which was perhaps only to be expected at that time. Reading through these letters was very difficult for me. True, they were old letters, by nearly ten years, dating from just after the last time we had seen each other, just after we had agreed to marry, and they spanned a period of nearly two years.

What emerged from these letters was that Eugene had done everything he said he would:

he had found a house, arranged a course at Edinburgh University for me, and even arranged a small stipend from a Polish émigré organisation. But the letters were increasingly pained. He could not understand why I did not reply. Of course, by the time he was writing the last of these letters, I had not heard from him for nearly two years. I had become so angry at what I took to be his failure that I had taken up with someone else. I was actually living with another man. Perhaps I did this out of spite. Well, maybe. My relationship with this other man did not last anyway, and his promise of marriage came to nothing either.

But the real secret of Eugene's letters almost escaped me. Inside the plastic bag the letters were bundled together with elastic bands. I found a small piece of paper trapped in one of the bundles. It was an official slip, beautifully printed on expensive card. It read: 'Courtesy of Her Britannic Majesty's Embassy, Consular/Visa Section, Warsaw'. That was all. I was puzzled. What was this doing in with my letters?

I asked my father. He thought about it for a while, consulted a couple of friends, then said that in his opinion the Polish Post Office had sent the package to me because they were clearing up a backlog of matters from the communist years. These letters had been intercepted at the Warsaw sorting office, by the Security Service, handed over to the British Embassy, kept for a while, then returned to the

Security Service. The Post Office, by simply returning the letters in a plastic wallet, by not removing the Embassy slip, was making it quite clear they had no hand in the arrangements.

My father said it was no secret that I was planning to marry. No secret I was planning to leave the country. Of course the British could not have done this without the cooperation of the Security Service and the Party. But we have to be clear about this. It was not the Party that stopped me going to Britain. It was the British Embassy. My father, an ex-Party member, says this must be the case. I also think, now, that it must be so. Neither the Party nor the British wanted me to leave Poland. They connived to prevent it by hijacking Eugene's letters until our relationship broke down. I wanted to write to Eugene to say I understood, finally, what had happened, that it was not his fault. But by this time I had no way of contacting him.

Several times Eugene said to me: 'OK, so you don't like communism. But you really don't want what we have in the West either. You just don't know that yet.' This used to puzzle and irritate me. Now, after the collapse of communism, after ten years of 'freedom', 'the market', 'democracy' and 'capitalism', I can see that we have simply replaced one style of greed and chaos with another. I think I understand what he meant. I have wanted for some time to say these things to him. Perhaps

when you find him, you will say them for me.
That is all.

It is interesting that her version of their final meeting differs from his account: he says she would have nothing to do with him, she says they agreed to marry.

With this letter we are brought back to the title of this work and the personal tragedy - one of many - that haunts every political event. The title, *Burning Worm,* derives from one of Hinks' offbeat little poems: '*Another kink in the rope, It strains to stay straight But another kink in the rope And it turns it twists It writhes like a burning worm*'. In this one vivid image, Hinks speaks of the stress of being caught up in a massively important political event, but at the same time captures the agony of unresolved personal issues.

Prof Dr S.Mroz
Jagiellonian University
Kraków
Poland
15 August 2001

chronology

August 1980

14 16,000 workers at Lenin Shipyard Gdańsk strike over pay and conditions. Next day 40,000 workers in the region join the strike. Within a week 260 industrial enterprises are on strike, and an inter-factory strike is committee.

23 Deputy Premier Jagielski arrives at the shipyards to negotiate a settlement.

26 Inter-factory strike committee numbers over 1,000 delegates. Strikes begin in Silesia.

31 Government and strikers sign an agreement.

September 1980

5 At a late night Central Committee meeting, Stanislaw Kania replaces Edward Gierek - rumoured to be in hospital with heart trouble - as First Secretary of the Party. Kania had previously been in charge of the army, security service and relations with the Church.

24 Solidarność attempts to register union statutes in court but meets with unexplained delays.

October 1980

3 In protest at the delay in the courts Solidarność organises a national one-hour warning strike.

24 Court insists union statutes must acknowledge the leading role of the Party. Union threatens a general strike.

29 East Germany closes border with Poland.

November 1980

10 Court agrees to accept registration of the union with statutes unchanged.

December 1980

1 Soviet military maneuvers on the Polish-Ukrainian border.

5   Warsaw Pact summit meeting in Moscow.
8   NATO claims Warsaw Pact forces fully deployed along Polish borders.
14 Farmers gather in Warsaw to demand registration of Rural Solidarność.
31 Poland's international debt is $23,000,000,000.

January 1981
2   Peasant occupation-strike begins in Rzeszów.
24 Solidarność instructs members not to work Saturdays.
27 Farmers in Rzeszów occupy Agriculture Ministry offices demanding recognition for Rural Solidarność.
28 General strike in Bielsko Biała province begins.

February 1981
3   National strike called off as government agrees to negotiate over Rural Solidarność.
9   Defence Minister General Jaruzelski becomes Prime Minister, and immediately suggests a 90-day truce. Solidarność agrees. General Strike in Jelenia Góra.
17 Student Solidarność recognised.
18 Rzeszów occupation ends.

March 1981
19 Milicja disrupt local council meeting in Bydgoszcz, beat-up several Solidarność activists.
20 Warsaw Pact maneuvers begin on Polish border. Solidarność threatens a strike unless those responsible for the beatings in Bydgoszcz are brought to justice.
27 National four-hour warning strike
31 Lech Wałęsa and the government reach a private agreement. Without consulting the union Wałęsa calls off the threatened national strike.

April 1981
1   Criticism of Wałęsa: several Solidarność leaders resign. Meat rationing introduced.

26   Poland's International debt $25,000,000,000.

May 1981
12   Rural Solidarność registered with courts.
28   Cardinal Wyszyński dies.

June 1981
9   Soviet leadership sends a warning letter to the Polish leadership.

July 1981
7   Bishop Glemp nominated as successor to Wyszyński.
14   Extraordinary Party Congress.
25   Hunger marches throughout Poland.

August 1981
6   Talks between Government and Solidarność break down. Motorcades block Warsaw streets in protest.
31   Solidarność membership reaches 10 million.

September 1981
4   Soviet naval maneuvers start in the bay of Gdańsk.
10   Solidarność First National Congress in Gdańsk sends a message of support to all independent trades unionists in the Soviet bloc.
11   Moscow describes Solidarność Congress as a provocation and an orgy of anti-socialism.
12   Polish Communist Party leaks a threatening letter from Moscow.

October 1981
4   Steep price increases in food and tobacco, unleashing a wave of wildcat strikes.
15   Government suspends price increases.
18   First Secretary Kania is replaced by General Jaruzelski who proposes a ban on strikes.
19   Wałęsa opposes proposed ban.

23 Jaruzelski sends three-man army units into the countryside to help rural officials procure food and control the black market.

28 One-hour national warning strike.

November 1981

4 Summit meeting between Glemp, Jaruzelski and Wałęsa.

7 160,000 on strike in Zielona Góra.

9 Solidarność invited to take part in Government of National Accord.

12 Zielona Góra strike ends. 125,000 workers still on strike in various parts of Poland.

17 Talks between Government and Solidarność reach stalemate.

23 Fifteen leading members of Solidarność resign in protest at Wałęsa's conciliatory attitude towards the government.

24 Soviet Marshal Kulikov visits Warsaw for talks with Jaruzelski.

28 Sixth Plenum of Polish Party Central Committee demands a Special Powers Bill.

December 1981

1 Warsaw Pact Defence Ministers meet in Warsaw.

2 Helicopters and riot police break up strike of cadets at Warsaw Fire Officers Academy.

5 University Day of Protest: 70 universities strike.

6 Solidarność Day of Protest in response to events of 2 December.

7 Warsaw radio broadcasts tape of Solidarność meeting where the overthrow of the regime is discussed.

10 Moscow sends another angry letter to Polish leadership.

11 Solidarność National Commission convenes in Gdańsk, calling for free elections and a referendum on the conduct of the government.

13 Jaruzelski declares Martial Law and suspends both Solidarność and the Communist Party.

Burning Worm

acknowledgments

parts of this novel have appeared in:
The Big Issue, Planet, Arcade, The Edmonton Journal,
Frames, Poetry Wales and *Metropolitan;*
Andrzej D, Lucy and *April Fool*
have been broadcast on BBC Radio 4

financial assistance from The Royal Literary Society, the
K.Blundel Trust, and North West Arts Board is gratefully
acknowledged

thanks for support and good fellowship to:
Mariola Żychowska, Jane Stupnicka, Marta Sawicka,
Patrick Fletcher, Olga Hubicka, Loraine Zamorska, Chris
& Danusia Scott-Barrett, Ela Jarosz, Ewa Szary, Ewa
Pałka, Bill Brand, Krysia Bławat, Margaret Marchment,
Neil Jones, Elizabeth Baines, John Ashbrook, Dave, Anne
& Grace Downes, Maggie Watt, Roger Prat, Norman
Leach, Barbara Binns, Frankie Hudson, David Emerson,
Mick & Pat O'Rourke, Des Smith, Corine Deliot, Cathie
& Tony Gard, Mary Niesłuchowska, Tadek & Halina
Orłowsci, Brian & Linda Pawłowska-Wasileski, Yvonne
Lyon, Shirley Franklin, Corine Ferry, Trevor Greenley,
Danuta Depa, Ela Perepeczko, Dorota Kaniak, Jon
Preece, Oliver Reynolds, Wil Roberts, Ned Thomas, John
Tripp, John Osmond, Nigel Jenkins, Nick Fry,
Madeleine & Luke Rose